The Little Tragedies

Russian Literature and Thought

Gary Saul Morson, series editor

The Little Tragedies

ALEXANDER PUSHKIN

Translated, with Critical Essays, by Nancy K. Anderson

Yale University Press ❀ New Haven and London

Designed by Rebecca Gibb.

Set in Fournier type by Tseng Information Systems.

Printed in the United States of America.

Library of Congress Cataloging-in-Publication Data

Pushkin, Aleksandr Sergeevich, 1799–1837.

[Malen'kie tragedii. English]

The little tragedies / Alexander Pushkin ; translated, with critical essays, by Nancy K. Anderson.

p. cm. — (Russian literature and thought)

Includes bibliographical references and index.

ISBN 0-300-08025-5 (cloth : alk. paper) — ISBN 0-300-08027-1 (pbk. : alk. paper)

1. Pushkin, Aleksandr Sergeevich, 1799–1837 — Translations into English. I. Title. II. Series. III. Anderson, Nancy K.

PG3347 .A2 2000

891.72′3 21 — dc21

99–046416

A catalogue record for this book is available from the British Library.

The paper in this book meets the guidelines for permanence and durability of the Committee on Production Guidelines for Book Longevity of the Council on Library Resources.

10 9 8 7 6 5 4 3 2 1

Contents

Acknowledgments

I WOULD LIKE to express my gratitude to Robert L. Jackson of Yale University for his continuing advice and encouragement during the process of writing this book; and to Caryl Emerson of Princeton University for her sensitive reading of, and valuable corrections to, the translations.

The illustrations are by Vladimir Favorsky from a Soviet edition of the "little tragedies."

Introduction

So far I've been reading nothing but Pushkin and am drunk
with rapture, every day I discover something new.

Fyodor Dostoevsky in a letter to his wife, 16 (28) July 1874

IF ONE ASKED a Russian to name Russia's greatest writer, the un-
hesitating reply would be not Dostoevsky or Tolstoy but Pushkin. Yet
an English-speaking reader who is not a Slavist probably knows little
of Pushkin's work beyond *Eugene Onegin* — if, indeed, he or she recognizes the name of Pushkin at all. Thus, a translation of Pushkin's
"little tragedies" to the English-speaking public requires a few words
placing the work in its context.

The "little tragedies" is the name traditionally given to the collection of Pushkin's four short dramas in verse, *The Miserly Knight,
Mozart and Salieri, The Stone Guest,* and *A Feast During the Plague.*[1]
These four dramas were never published together in Pushkin's lifetime:
indeed, *The Stone Guest* was not printed until after his death. Never-

theless, the four plays clearly are united, not only by their common origin, but by their similar form and themes.

The plays were written in circumstances that themselves were highly dramatic. In 1830, Pushkin was thirty-one years old and regarded himself as having outlived his first youth and reached the time to settle down. He had become engaged to a young woman of great beauty and (by the nobility's standards) little money, Natalya Goncharova. At least he hoped he was engaged to her, for Natalya's mother unsentimentally regarded the marriage of her most eligible daughter as the means of settling her family's financial future in the best possible manner, and was conducting the marriage negotiations accordingly. Pushkin's status as a writer was of little help, since in the Russia of 1830 literature was regarded more as a gentlemanly hobby than a profession, which was reflected in writers' pay. In addition, Pushkin, like most adult sons of the Russian nobility, had not distinguished himself by his thrift, and the resulting quarrels with his father had done nothing to improve his financial position. But Pushkin's willingness to take on the adult obligation of marriage pleased his father, and to improve his position in the marriage negotiations, his father gave him a share of the family property of the village of Boldino, in the province of Nizhny Novgorod. At the beginning of September 1830, Pushkin arrived at Boldino, both to take possession and to find a place far enough from his potential mother-in-law so that he could maintain his emotional equilibrium and concentrate on his writing. He had also discovered, en route from Moscow, that he was going to be even more isolated in the country than he had thought: cholera had broken out there, and officials at post-horse stations along the way were encouraging travelers to turn back. In 1830, cholera was a mysterious, untreatable, sometimes fatal disease; but the on-again, off-again wedding negotiations had driven Pushkin to such a state of exasperation and fury that the risk actually appealed to him, and he pressed onward.

Thus in the autumn of 1830, Pushkin's past way of life clearly was coming to an end, whereas his future—assuming he lived to see it

—was thoroughly unpredictable; and in the solitude of the Russian countryside, with dirt roads washed out by the autumn rains and travel further restricted by quarantines, he had plenty of time for reflection. The result was an extraordinary burst of creativity, an artistic summation of everything that he had thought and experienced. In the three months that Pushkin spent at Boldino, he wrote the final canto of *Eugene Onegin,* along with two sections not included in the final version of that work (one on Onegin's travels and at least the beginning of a politically unpublishable "Canto X"); *The Little House in Kolomna,* a humorous anecdote in octaves; two mock folk tales in verse, *The Story of the Priest and His Workman Balda* and *The Story of the She-Bear;* some thirty lyric poems, ranging from polemics to elegies; *The Tales of Belkin,* five short stories which were Pushkin's first completed works of prose fiction, along with an incomplete story, *History of the Village of Goryukhino;* and four plays now referred to as the "little tragedies."

The completion date of each play is written on its manuscript: *The Miserly Knight* is dated 23 October 1830, *Mozart and Salieri* 26 October, *The Stone Guest* 4 November, and *A Feast During the Plague* 8 November. Behind this extraordinarily short time of composition, however, lay several years of reflection. An undated jotting of Pushkin's lists ten possible subjects for plays, among them *The Miser, Mozart and Salieri,* and *Don Juan;* judging from other notes on the same sheet of paper, this was probably written in 1826. From Pushkin's biography, one can see why these three subjects not only would have appealed to him originally, but would have stayed in his thoughts over the following years. Pushkin's financial dependence upon his money-conscious father had made him aware of the paradoxical relationship of money and personal freedom: too little money, and one's freedom of action was hemmed by external constraints; too much interest in money, and one's inner freedom was lost—an insight that was to find expression in *The Miserly Knight.* Pushkin's prolonged quarrels with untalented but officially favored "patriotic" writers had shown him the depth of malice that could be reached by professional envy; and such envy was to form the starting point for Pushkin's creation of Salieri, although Salieri is no more a "simple" envier than the Baron is a "simple" miser. As for Don Juan, Pushkin himself had a reputation in his youth as a ladies' man, and kept what he called a "Don Juan list" of his female conquests. As the marriage negotiations with Natalya Goncharova's mother dragged on, Pushkin developed a new idea of Don Juan, as the former womanizer who at last falls in love with a "good" woman and who desires her exclusive faithfulness so passionately that he feels jealous even of her dead husband. Doña Anna becomes a young and beautiful widow, still feeling affection toward the memory of the husband whom she married at her mother's command, but not ready to be faithful to that memory for the rest of her life—the very position in which Pushkin, with horror, imagined a widowed Natalya one day finding herself.[2] Anna Akhmatova has suggested that it was the intensely personal nature of *The Stone Guest* that made Pushkin decide against publishing it in his lifetime. *A Feast During the Plague,* as its absence from Pushkin's jotting shows, has a different origin from the other three plays. It is a translation, with significant modifications by Pushkin, of a scene from a much longer work, *The City of the Plague,* written by a minor English contemporary of Pushkin's, John Wilson. Pushkin's copy of this work, which he took to Boldino with him, was published in 1829; it no doubt evoked memories of Pushkin's visit to the Caucasus in that year, during which he witnessed an outbreak of the plague in Erzrum, the capital of Armenia. The cholera epidemic raging in the countryside around Boldino in 1830 made the topic even more grimly appropriate.

But the "little tragedies" are not merely artistic transformations of Pushkin's own personal experience. They also reflect his interest in the potential of drama as a means of exploring human passions. Each of the "little tragedies" has a protagonist of such exceptional gifts and strength of character that he dominates all the people and circumstances surrounding him. The internal psychological conflict of this central character, who faces a crucial choice between opposing alternatives, thus becomes the key plot element. This is most obvious in *The Miserly Knight*, where the conflict of the central character is summarized in its very title, and in *A Feast During the Plague*, where Walsingham uses his dominant position as chairman to turn the feast into an ongoing discussion of the issue that obsesses him, the relation of the living and the dead. In *Mozart and Salieri* this key plot element assumes an unexpected form: the genius Mozart appears as a secondary figure, while the play is dominated by the inner drama of the lesser composer Salieri, who is torn between his love of Mozart's music and the ambition and envy that makes him sentence Mozart to death. In *The Stone Guest*, the conflict involves two extreme types of relationship between a man and a woman: one emphasizing the beauty and ecstasy of the moment, with no expectation beyond that; the other emphasizing the constancy of love, throughout life and even beyond the grave.

Passion, choice, consequences — these were the issues to which, at a crucial moment in his own life, Pushkin's thoughts and imagination turned. Free will and fate, for him, were not opposites. Rather, they were organically linked, jointly expressing what Pushkin saw as the great moral law: the law of Nemesis, that a given choice carries a particular payment or reward as its inevitable result, that "as a man sows, so shall he reap." What unites the four protagonists of the "little tragedies" is that each of them is impelled by a dominating passion to violate the moral law, and, as the penalty for that violation, loses the very thing he sought to gain. The Baron loses both his knightly honor and his hoarded treasure, which, as he has foreseen with horror, will pass to his spendthrift son. Salieri murders Mozart in the name of Art, only to face the gnawing suspicion that he, the would-be genius, is in fact no better than the common crowd. Don Juan, who was ready to gamble his life for Doña Anna's love, loses both her and his life. Walsingham, who cherishes his late wife's image of him as "proud and free," displays that pride and freedom in an inhuman manner and is forced to acknowledge that he is ashamed before "her immortal eyes." The consistent affirmation of the retribution that occurs when moral law is violated by a destructive passion — a retribution that transcends all the differences in the centuries, cultures, and individual characters depicted in each play — evokes two lines that Pushkin had written years before in *The Gypsies:*

И всюду страсти роковые,
И от судеб защити нет.

[And everywhere are fatal passions;
Against the Fates there's no defense.]

This emphasis on the fateful choice of a central figure is the key to not only the plot, but the structure of the "little tragedies." Everything that could distract attention from the fundamental element is swept away. The number of characters is reduced to a minimum: indeed, in *Mozart and Salieri* the title characters are the only two speaking parts. Moreover, the noncentral characters do not exist independently; they are defined by their relationship to the central character, either as opposites (as Mozart is to Salieri, or as Mary's song is to Walsingham's song) or as "doubles" (as the Jewish moneylender and the Duke both echo aspects of the Baron's personality, or as Laura is a female counterpart to Don Juan). The action is likewise reduced to the most essential elements. In contrast to a traditional play, in which the largest part of the drama is spent in developing the conflict or plot complication which is resolved only at the end, each of the "little tragedies" starts, so to speak, at the beginning of the fifth act, at the moment when a preexisting unstable situation is at the point of becoming a crisis, and moves swiftly and inexorably to its catastrophic climax.

The "little tragedies" contain a number of scenes that are so intensely dramatic that they demand to be seen and heard, rather than merely read: the Baron's monologue in *The Miserly Knight,* or the ever-deepening horror of the conversation between the murderer and his victim in the second scene of *Mozart and Salieri,* or the tangle of wariness and attraction, passion and calculation, between Don Juan and Doña Anna in the last scene of *The Stone Guest*. But despite the obviously dramatic nature of the plays, they present serious problems in production. Three of the four plays contain music that is to be performed by a character; and although it could be argued that Laura's songs in *The Stone Guest* are episodic and not fundamentally different in their dramatic function from the songs that occur in so many of Shakespeare's plays, the performances by Mozart in *Mozart and Salieri* and the songs of Mary and Walsingham in *A Feast During the Plague* are as important in the plays as the spoken dialogue. No less than the words, this music is an expression of the deepest feelings, the worldview, of the performer, and is perceived as such by the other characters, who respond to it accordingly. And yet Pushkin provides no practical directions for the music. The piece that Mozart plays in the first scene is not even identified. His performance in the second is described only as being from the *Requiem;* that is, one man is playing on a piano (and possibly also singing) a selection from a work which is scored for four voices, chorus, and orchestra, while preserving the majesty of the original—a transcription problem worthy of Liszt. Mary's and Walsingham's songs are both mere lyrics not set to any melody, although the choice of music would be a crucial factor in the songs' effect.

The degree to which Pushkin left such a vital production feature undelineated raises the question: did the author envision the plays being staged, and if so, how? One alternative may be ruled out immediately: as an avid theatergoer who had had many occasions to observe audience behavior, Pushkin cannot have regarded the "little tragedies" as stageable in a conventional commercial theater. It has often been pointed out that no commercial playwright would state an important theme of the play in its very first two lines, as Pushkin does with Salieri's monologue ("They say there's no justice here on earth, / But there's no justice higher up, either"). During the first five minutes latecomers will still be arriving and people still getting settled in their seats, and the playwright must adjust the weight of the opening lines accordingly. But what makes the "little tragedies" unstageable in a conventional theater is not just one or another specific problem, but the very nature of the plays. Because they are stripped so completely to their essentials, not only every word but every breath, every facial expression, acquires a relative importance far greater than in a conventional play. And in proportion, the ordinary problems which regularly diminish the perception of a member of a play's audience — a coughing spectator, a poor seat — become far more seriously damaging to the work's reception.

The "little tragedies" thus must have been intended for a small audience in an intimate setting, a dramatic equivalent of chamber music. The chamber music analogy also suggests one way in which Pushkin might have imagined the plays being performed. Chamber music was often written to be played not only by professional musicians, but also by gifted amateurs (Beethoven's Archduke Trio and Schubert's "Trout" Quintet, to mention two well-known examples, both contain parts designed to be played by the patrons who had commissioned the works). The more cultivated members of the Russian aristocracy, which produced gifted amateurs in many artistic fields, would certainly have been capable of participating in such a "chamber theater." Indeed, in the 1890s, the young and as-yet-unknown poet Alexander Blok courted his future wife, Lyubov Mendeleyeva, during the amateur theatricals that were staged in the summer at her family's estate, where a converted barn was equipped with a stage, footlights, and benches for the spectators; family friends would long remember Blok's performance as Hamlet to Mendeleyeva's Ophelia. In 1899, in honor of the centennial of Pushkin's birth, this little theater staged scenes from *Boris Godunov, The Miserly Knight,* and *The Stone Guest.* It may well be that the best nineteenth-century performances of the "little tragedies" occurred in precisely such private settings and have now vanished without trace, save for a diary entry or a line in a yellowing letter.

How then should the "little tragedies" be staged for an audience today? An experimental theater is, of course, one option; but given the small number of such theaters, a more accessible forum would be desirable. The twentieth century has in fact provided such a medium — film. The intimacy of the "little tragedies" is precisely suited to a medium capable of close-up shots and of continually positioning the audience at the best possible viewing angle — a medium that, in addition, has traditionally integrated drama with music. Indeed, the "little tragedies" seem so much better adapted to film than to live theater that one is tempted to suggest that the reason Pushkin left crucial aspects of the performance undescribed in his manuscript is because he realized that he was pushing beyond the staging capabilities of his day, creating works that would require twentieth- or even twenty-first-century technology to produce their full effect.

Even as unstaged scripts, however, the four plays have long been recognized as among the greatest works of Russia's greatest writer. Dostoevsky was fascinated by the image of the miserly knight: in an article dated 1861, "Petersburg Dreams in Verse and Prose," he explicitly acknowledged its influence on his early short story "Mr. Prokharchin"; fourteen years later he created Arkady Dolgoruky, the central character of *The Adolescent*, an embittered youth preoccupied with thoughts of gaining wealth and power (what he calls "the idea of Rothschild") who has learned the Baron's monologue by heart and regards it as representing the greatest idea Pushkin ever expressed. For D. S. Mirsky, author of perhaps the definitive one-volume history of Russian literature in the English language, *The Stone Guest* is one of two works (the other being *The Bronze Horseman*) jointly "claiming the first place in Russian poetry." [3] Without professing to rival the perfection of Pushkin's verse — a task before which the boldest translator would quail — I hope, nevertheless, that this translation will at last make the "little tragedies" readily accessible to English speakers, and thus help to give these four extraordinary plays the recognition they deserve as masterpieces not merely of Russian, but of world literature.

The Little Tragedies in English:
An Approach

NONE OF PUSHKIN'S WORK is so well known to English speakers as it should be, but the "little tragedies" are particularly underrepresented. In contrast to, for example, *Eugene Onegin*, of which several fairly good translations are available in English, translations of the "little tragedies" are few and frequently do not include all four plays.[1] The reason translators largely avoid these works, I believe, is because of the difficulty in handling what in modern English literature is a completely disused genre, the drama in blank verse. T. S. Eliot, who strove to revive the form in his plays (*Murder in the Cathedral, The Family Reunion, The Cocktail Party*), has described the problems he encountered in writing a verse drama in two essays, *Poetry and Drama* and

The Music of Poetry. These essays have a number of valuable insights to offer the would-be translator of the "little tragedies."

Poetry and Drama addresses the questions of whether and how poetry could be used in a modern English play:

> Whether we use prose or verse on the stage, they are both but means to an end. The difference, from one point of view, is not so great as we might think. In those prose plays which survive, which are read and produced on the stage by later generations, the prose which the characters speak is as remote, for the best part, from the vocabulary, syntax and rhythm of our ordinary speech — with its fumbling for words, its constant recourse to approximation, its disorder and its unfinished sentences — as verse is. Like verse, it has been written, and rewritten. . . . I mean to draw a triple distinction: between prose, and verse, and our ordinary speech which is mostly below the level of either verse or prose. So if you look at it this way, it will appear that prose, on the stage, is as artificial as verse: or alternatively, that verse can be as natural as prose.[2]

Thus, for Eliot, the appropriate language for a play is not that which is most like how we speak, but that which is most like how we would speak if we could do so. It is idealized language, but to be dramatically convincing, it must be an idealization of the actual speech of its time. Moreover, because most of life is taken up with what we revealingly call prosaic matters, in most cases the appropriate language for the action of a play will be either prose or, if it is verse, verse that has no particularly great merit as poetry. Poetry should be used "only . . . when the dramatic situation has reached such a point of intensity that poetry becomes the natural utterance, because then it is the only language in which the emotions can be expressed at all."[3]

One sees the logic of this argument by considering the difference between poetry and prose. Poetry may be described as a cross between prose and music. Both prose and music evoke emotion, but in different ways. Prose evokes an emotion in a particular context; music evokes emotion directly, without specifying the circumstance that gives rise to the emotion. In prose, a person may be joyous because he has fallen in love, or achieved a long-sought goal, or simply seen a cherry tree in bloom; but in any case, there is a stated cause for joy. Music conveys only the joy itself, although an individual hearer may associate a particular piece of music with a specific joyous event. Poetry, to the extent that it is akin to prose, evokes an emotion for a stated reason; but to the extent that it is akin to music, it evokes a more intense emotion than can be explained simply by pointing to the stated reason. When compared to prose, poetry has an emotional surcharge. It was this surcharge of which Lermontov was thinking when he wrote:

Есть речи — значенье
Темно иль ничтожно,
Но им без волненья
Внимать невозможно.

[There are speeches whose meaning is obscure or of no import, but it is impossible to hear them without being moved.]

This emotional surcharge explains why nonpoets traditionally try to write poetry at moments of great emotional intensity, such as during first love or in wartime: they instinctively realize that this is the form capable of accommodating the greatest emotional content. This is also why in works like Shakespeare's tragedies or Pushkin's *Boris Godunov,* where prose and poetry are mixed, the prose is used for the more "everyday" speech of the characters, whereas the great setpiece monologues — the emotional peaks of the work — are in poetry.

It follows, then, that a work like any of the "little tragedies," in which a pure emotional peak is sustained for the entire length of the work, can only be written in — and translated as — poetry. But having reached this conclusion, the translator then encounters a problem thus described by Eliot in *The Music of Poetry:*

> The history of blank verse illustrates two interesting and related points: the dependence upon speech and the striking difference, in what is prosodically the same form, between dramatic blank verse and blank verse employed for epical, philosophical, meditative and idyllic purposes. The dependence of verse upon speech is much more direct in dramatic poetry than in any other. In most kinds of poetry, the necessity for its reminding us of contemporary speech is reduced by the latitude allowed for personal idiosyncrasy. . . . But in dramatic verse the poet is speaking in one character after another, through the medium of a company of actors trained by a prducer, and of different actors and different producers at different times: his idiom must be comprehensive of all the voices, but present at a deeper level than is necessary when the poet speaks only for himself. Some of Shakespeare's later verse is very elaborate and peculiar: but it remains the language, not of one person, but of a world of persons. . . . By the time of Otway dramatic blank verse has become artificial and at best reminiscent; and when we get to the verse plays by nineteenth century poets, of which the greatest is probably *The Cenci*, it is difficult to preserve any illusion of reality. Nearly all the greater poets of the last century tried their hands at verse plays. These plays, which few people read more than once, are treated with respect as fine poetry; and their insipidity is usually attributed to the fact that the authors, though great poets, were amateurs in the theatre. But even if the poets had had greater natural gifts for the theatre, or had toiled to acquire the craft, their plays would have been just as ineffective, unless their theatrical talent had shown them the necessity for a different kind of versification. It is not primarily lack of plot, or lack of action and suspense, or im-

perfect realization of character, or lack of anything of what is called "theatre," that makes these plays so lifeless: it is primarily that their rhythm of speech is something that we cannot associate with any human being except a poetry reader.[4]

Eliot does not profess to be able to explain fully why it was that although blank verse was properly rooted in the speech of society as a whole, and thus capable of being believably used in a drama with a wide range of characters, in the time of Shakespeare, it had lost such roots by the time of Browning and Tennyson. But he does suggest that a major factor was the influence of Milton:

> I should not care to advance any one reason why prose came to supersede verse in the theatre. But I feel sure that one reason why blank verse cannot be employed now in the drama is that so much non-dramatic poetry, and great non-dramatic poetry, has been written in it in the last three hundred years. . . . If we can imagine, as a flight of fancy, Milton coming before Shakespeare, Shakespeare would have had to discover quite a different medium from that which he used and perfected. Milton handled blank verse in a way which no one has ever approached or will ever approach: and in so doing did more than anyone or anything else to make it impossible for the drama: though we may also believe that dramatic blank verse had exhausted its resources, and had no future in any event. Indeed, Milton almost made blank verse impossible for any purpose for a couple of generations. It was the precursors of Wordsworth—Thomson, Young, Cowper—who made the first efforts to rescue it from the degradation to which the eighteenth-century imitators of Milton had reduced it.[5]

Eliot, then, sees Milton as a cosmic force exerting a gravitational field so powerful that for a time all English blank verse—both lyric and dramatic—is forced into orbit around him. By the time of Wordsworth, lyric blank verse had liberated itself from his overpowering effect and reconnected itself to the common spoken language of its day. But dramatic blank verse—perhaps already weakened by other, subtle factors—never achieved a similar liberation and reconnection. And yet such a connection with the spoken language of its day is most vital precisely in dramatic poetry, with its requirement that a range of characters speak in a manner appropriate to their natures.

Applying Eliot's insights, one can see why English translations of the "little tragedies" are so few and often only partially successful. The translator is on the horns of a dilemma: if a translation is in prose, the added emotional effect associated with a poetic translation is lost; if a translation is in blank verse, the distance between the cadence of dramatic blank verse and that of the modern English language is so great that the reader or listener finds it impossible to believe that such a speech is an outpouring of the speaker's heart.

What, then, is a would-be translator to do? I have no theoretical solution to offer, but I do have an empirical one. I have attempted to translate the "little tragedies" into language that, first, is vivid and modern enough to sound credible to a reader or listener and engage the emotions, and then to make that language as musical as it can possibly be made before losing its credibility. The result turned out to be what might be called a "semi-metrical" translation: its lines have a strong but not invariable tendency to be divisible into two-syllable feet, and their average length is around ten syllables, although individual lines may vary from six to fourteen syllables. Although it is not Pushkin's iambic pentameter, it is haunted by the ghost of that meter. But this suggestive similarity—sometimes quite striking, sometimes much fainter—was not what I consciously set out to produce; I merely wanted a language that was as compelling as possible. Intensity, more than anything else, is what the "little tragedies" are about. The reader or listener should be on the edge of his seat during them. Every means I could find to convey this intensity I have used; any form or device which diminishes it I have avoided. My principle has been that enunciated by A. K. Tolstoy in his translation of Goethe's *Die Braut von Korinth* and cited approvingly by Korney Chukovsky in his study of translation:

> I am trying . . . as much as is possible, to be faithful to the original, but only when fidelity or exactness does not damage the artistic impression, and, without hesitating for a minute, I am deviating from a literal translation if that may produce a different impression in Russian than in German.
>
> I think that it's not necessary to translate the words and sometimes not even the meaning; the important thing is, one has to convey the impression.
>
> The reader of the translation has to be transported into the same sphere in which the reader of the original finds himself; the translation has to act on the same nerves.[6]

Chukovsky explicitly extends this principle to translating into a different meter when the original meter is culturally inappropriate in the target language:

> Into what meter, for example, should Lermontov's poetry be translated by Uzbeks, since for them the iambic tetrameter is an exoticism, something completely foreign to their system of poetics? In this case, equirhythmic translation would be unthinkable, because the rich, subtle and complex poetic tradition of the Uzbeks has no place for iambic tetrameter, and the Uzbeks, who over many centuries have accumulated enormous poetic experience, perceive a European verse form in a completely different manner than we do. When it came to, for example, translating Lermontov's "Hadji Abrek" into Uzbek, two outstanding Uzbek poets, Gafur Guliam and Sheikh-zade, didn't even try to translate it into the same meter, because to

an Uzbek's ear that is not equivalent to the impression which that same iamb produces on a Russian ear. Thus Gafur Guliam translated Lermontov's iambic tetrameter into a thirteen-syllable "barmak" line (that is, into syllabic verse), and Sheikh-zade into a nine-syllable "barmak" line; and viewed against the traditional background of Uzbek poetry, this is the equivalent of iambic tetrameter.[7]

On the strength of Chukovsky's argument alone, even without regard for the particular problem presented by dramatic blank verse, one could make a case for a "semi-metrical" rather than strictly metrical translation of the "little tragedies." Contemporary poetry in English has moved so far toward free verse (still a rarity in Russian) that a strictly metrical translation sounds "dated" or "bookish" to a modern English speaker in the way that the original does not to a modern Russian speaker.

Metrics, however, are not the only problem encountered in conveying an adequate impression of the "little tragedies." The vocabulary, too, needs to be sufficiently contemporary and forceful. To give an example: the Baron's second-scene monologue in *The Miserly Knight* begins in Russian with the words:

Как молодой повеса ждет свиданья
С какой-нибудь развратницей лукавой
Иль дурой, им обманутой, так я
Весь день минуты ждал, когда сойду
В подвал мой тайный, к верным сундукам.

In A. F. B. Clark's translation this becomes:

As some young scapegrace bides the trysting hour
With some corrupt enchantress or perchance
Some foolish girl seduced by him, so I

> All day abide the time when I shall come
> Down to my secret vault and trusty chests.

In Nabokov's translation this reads:

> Just as a mad young fellow frets awaiting
> his rendez-vous with some evasive harlot,
> or with the goose seduced by him, thus I
> have dreamt all day of coming down at last
> in vaulted dimness to my secret chests.

And in Eugene M. Kayden's translation:

> As a young scamp who waits the trysting hour
> With some intriguing harlot or little fool
> He has seduced, thus I await daylong
> And dream of going down at last into
> This vaulted darkness to my secret chests.

Clark's "As some young scapegrace bides the trysting hour," although understandable on the printed page, has parted company with anything believable as spoken English. It simply slides by without catching on anything, without ever engaging either one's ear or one's emotions. Kayden, too, clearly is not hearing his own translation, or he would not introduce line breaks in places where they inappropriately split what should be a single thought—"little fool / He has seduced" and "into / This vaulted darkness." Nabokov's text is the one we can most readily imagine in a spoken voice—with the significant proviso that it should be a British upper-class voice. His rendering of дура as "goose" is a particularly striking touch, suggesting the dismissive contempt that a male aristocrat might feel in contemplating a credulous servant girl, just as "mad young fellow," with its combination of censure and joviality, suggests a gentleman deploring, but not seriously alarmed by, the traditional privilege of well-born youth to sow wild oats. And while the vocabularies of both Nabokov and Kayden are on the whole more recognizably modern than that of Clark, this does not mean they avoid archaisms altogether. Indeed, one choice made by both of them is worse than any single word in Clark — that is, the translation of развратницей as "harlot," a word so totally outdated in English, and so strongly smelling of hellfire preachers quoting the King James Bible, that any attempt actually to use it as a term of contempt is likely to produce a snicker instead. Each of the three translators has his own idea of how to deal with лукавой, which describes someone shrewd enough always to know where the main chance is and unscrupulous enough always to grab for it: in *Boris Godunov,* a boyar responds to a particularly realpolitik speech of Shuisky's by calling him a лукавый царедворец — a Machiavellian courtier; the line of the Lord's Prayer which in English is "deliver us from evil," in Church Slavonic is избави нас от лукаваго. Nabokov's "evasive harlot" is far too weak; Clark's "corrupt enchantress" is closer, and Kayden's "intriguing harlot" closer still. Finally, all three translators make a significant omission from Pushkin's text. In Clark the Baron "all day abide(s) the time" when he will go down to his treasure vaults; in Nabokov he "has dreamt all day of coming down"; in Kayden he "await(s) daylong / And dream(s) of going down"; but in Pushkin he весь день минуты ждал — all day he has been waiting for the minute to go down. This word "minute" conveys the violence of the emotional shift that occurs as the Baron descends to the vault: suddenly, after all that time waiting, that time which elapses meaninglessly, without weight or significance — suddenly there bursts upon him that supreme minute when it becomes possible to consummate his desire.

Thus, while it is possible to form a general impression of the Baron's words from any of the three translations, none of them conveys the emotional intensity of the speaker's imagery. To get at this intensity, the translator must go, as it were, behind the words of the original work, to reach the feelings and images of which the words are an embodiment, and then find the words that a speaker of another language would use to embody those same feelings and images. What is the central image of the Baron's opening lines? A tawdry, purely physical affair between a man who — as Leporello in *The Stone Guest* would say — has had plenty of women and will have plenty more, and a woman who evokes such contempt in the speaker's mind that the only real question is whether she is more defective in morals or in brains. Modern English certainly has words for that image, but they are not words that stand on dignity:

> Like a young skirt-chaser who waits for when
> He'll meet his bimbo — some tramp on the make,
> Or some fool he's snowed — that's how all day
> I wait for the minute when I go down
> Into my secret vault, to my faithful chests.

One might object that such language, while forceful enough, is too coarse to be spoken by a nobleman. But the language is jarring because the image is jarring. The Baron himself, as his great monologue reveals, is profoundly aware of the shamefulness of his passion for gold. The Baron feels too passionately, and is too honest with himself, to try to find dignified words for what he knows is wrong.

From this example, someone might jump to the conclusion that when I urge that the "little tragedies" be translated into believable spoken language, I am thinking of what is traditionally referred to as "low" style. This is not the case. The appropriateness of a style — "high," "low," or anything in between — is the result of the subject being addressed and the addresser's attitude toward it. What characterizes believable spoken language is neither subject nor attitude, but cadence. A verbal creation can be described as believable spoken language when, even if it is encountered on a printed page, the reader can hear it (so to speak) in his "mind's ear," can feel the pace of delivery slowing or quickening, can recognize the pause for emphasis, the sudden explosion of emotion, the ironic aside. It is entirely possible for a work to be high in style and yet have the unmistakable cadence of spoken language—the obvious example, for an American, being Lincoln's Gettysburg Address or Second Inaugural Address. It is true that (for reasons both too lengthy and too controversial to discuss here) the high style has largely disappeared from contemporary spoken English. Thus, when a passage in the "little tragedies" clearly calls for the high style, the best the translator can do is to take the cadence of a noncontemporary example and remove any too-obvious archaisms—to aim for a style which is negatively contemporary (not actively jarring to contemporaries) rather than positively so (recognizable by contemporaries as their own).

This problem of translating high style occurs throughout *The Stone Guest*. The play draws heavily on the fact that it is set in sixteenth-century Spain. Undergirding its structure is the whole set of images that that time and place automatically bring to mind: on the one side, the stern militance of the Counter-Reformation, the combination of palace and monastery that was the Escurial, the power and terror of El Greco's distorted saints under a stormy sky; on the other side, the passion all the more reckless for being forbidden, the nighttime serenade, the rose dropped from the balcony, the secret meeting. It is a world of love and death, the red and the black, a larger-than-life world. And its inhabitants, naturally enough, speak a language that to us seems the wildest extravagance. To Doña Anna it is not really surprising that an unknown man should throw himself on his knees before her and answer her question, "What do you want?" ("чего вы требуете?") with the speech:

> Смерть.
> О пусть умру сейчас у ваших ног,
> Пусть бедный прах мой здесь же похоронят
> Не подле праха, милого для вас,
> Не тут—не близко—дале где-нибудь,
> Там—у дверей—у самого порога,

Чтоб камня моего могли коснуться
Вы легкою ногой или одеждой,
Когда сюда, на этот гордый гроб,
Пойдете кудри наклонять и плакать.

To find a similar degree of extravagance in English poetry, one would have to go back several centuries—say, to Marvell's "To His Coy Mistress":

Had we but world enough, and time,
This coyness, Lady, were no crime.
We would sit down and think which way
To walk and pass our long love's day . . .
An hundred years should go to praise
Thine eyes and on thy forehead gaze;
Two hundred to adore each breast;
But thirty thousand to the rest;
An age at least to every part,
And the last age should show your heart;
For, Lady, you deserve this state,
Nor would I love at lower rate . . .

To be sure, Marvell is not an ideal model for Don Juan's speeches, because unlike Don Juan, he has a perfect sense of linguistic balance: he can simultaneously use the most extravagant language and smile at his own extravagance, and this contradiction not only does not destroy his literary artifice, but enhances our pleasure in it as we recognize the skill involved. In this sense of balance, the character who is most like Marvell is the First Guest at Laura's supper, with his ability to turn a perfectly mannered compliment for Laura's song:

Благодарим, волшебница. Ты сердце
Чаруешь нам. Из наслаждений жизни

Одной любви музыка уступает;
Но и любовь мелодия . . .

[Our thanks, enchantress. With your spells
You charm our hearts. Among life's pleasures
Music yields to none save love;
But love itself is melody . . .]

One realizes just from this beautiful and yet utterly impersonal speech
that the First Guest will go home safely that night, will pay a fashionable court to Laura or some other celebrated actress or dancer for a few
years, then will marry and settle down, and in his old age will horrify
and delight his grandchildren by telling them how he personally knew
that legendary reprobate, Don Juan.

But by subtracting Marvell's sense of balance—that sense which
necessarily makes a character not a protagonist but merely a First Guest
—while keeping Marvell's sense of extravagance, and using the result
not so much as a literal model for translation but as something which
was constantly and suggestively present while I was translating, as if it
were background music, I arrived at this version of Don Juan's speech:

Doña Anna: Well? What? What do you want?
Don Juan: To die.
              Oh, let me die this minute, at your feet.
              Let my poor dust be buried in this place,
              Not by the dust which is so dear to you,
              Nor anywhere nearby—some distance off,
              There—by the gates—at the very entrance,
              So when you come, my gravestone might be brushed
              By your light foot or by your dress's hem
              When you make your way to that proud grave
              To lay your ringlets on it and to weep.

One cannot point to any single detail in this translation that would be out of place in contemporary spoken English, and yet the speech as a whole has a decidedly "high," rhetorical tone—an echo, I hope, of that "courtly foreign grace" with which Tennyson imagined sixteenth-century Spaniards speaking.

In relying on the contemporary spoken language as the basis for a translation of the "little tragedies," I have followed Pushkin's own practice as a translator. One of the "little tragedies," *A Feast During the Plague,* is a modified translation by Pushkin of a single scene from a much longer English work, John Wilson's *City of the Plague.* Throughout this translation, Pushkin revises Wilson's style into a much less elaborate and more natural one (aside from any actual changes in meaning). Thus, in Wilson, Walsingham calls for Mary to sing in this manner:

> Sweet Mary Gray! Thou hast a silver voice,
> And wildly to thy native melodies
> Can tune its flute-like breath—sing us a song . . .

In Pushkin this becomes:

> Твой голос, милая, выводит звуки
> Родимых песен с диким совершенством;
> Спой, Мэри . . .

which I have translated as:

> Your voice, my dear, brings forth the songs
> Of your native land with rude perfection:
> Sing, Mary . . .

In Wilson, Louisa gives this account of her fainting:

I saw a horrid demon in my dream!
With sable visage and white-glaring eyes,
He beckon'd on me to ascend a cart
Filled with dead bodies . . .

In Pushkin this becomes:

> Ужасный демон
> Приснился мне: весь черный, белоглазный . . .
> Он звал меня в свою тележку. В ней
> Лежали мертвые . . .

which I have translated as:

> I dreamed I saw
> A hideous demon, black all over, with white eyes . . .
> He called me to his wagon. Lying in it
> Were the dead . . .

In Wilson, Walsingham's reply to the priest begins:

Why cam'st thou hither to disturb me thus?
I may not, must not go! Here am I held
By hopelessness in dark futurity,
By dire remembrance of the past — by hatred
And deep contempt of my own worthless self . . .

In Pushkin this becomes:

> Зачем приходишь ты
> Меня тревожить? Не могу, не должен
> Я за тобой идти: я здесь удержан

Отчаяньем, воспоминаньем страшным,
Сознаньем беззаконья моего . . .

which I have translated as:

> Why have you come here
> To trouble me? I cannot, I must not
> Follow after you: I am bound here
> By despair, by terrible remembrance,
> By the knowledge of my lawlessness . . .

In comparing Pushkin and Wilson, another aspect of Pushkin's ability as an author and translator specifically of dramatic poetry should be noted. For a drama in poetry to succeed, it must be successful both as poetry and as drama: that is, not only must the individual lines be good as poetry, but they must be psychologically appropriate to the character by whom they are spoken. Wilson makes no effort whatsoever to give any of his characters a recognizably individual voice. Part of this, no doubt, was simply the result of the overall design of his work, which might be described as a meditation on the horrors of the Plague and the consolations of faith. *The City of the Plague* has only the slenderest of narrative threads, and with its constantly changing scenes, it seems as dizzyingly overcrowded with figures as a Brueghel painting of a village wedding — although, in view of the grotesque treatment of its subject, a *Last Judgment* by Hieronymus Bosch might be a more appropriate comparison. In this sweeping view of the agony of a great city, it is perhaps understandable that Wilson does not expend too much energy on creating individually recognizable characters. What is surprising is that in contrast to the medieval paintings of the Dance of Death, where king and burgher, bishop and peasant, noblewoman and nun are all readily distinguishable, Wilson's characters do not even have voices appropriate to their social position. A sailor, a priest, a village girl, even the inevitable comic gravedigger, all speak in the same manner.

Unlike Wilson, Pushkin as an author of dramatic poetry was very conscious of the need for characters to speak a language suited to themselves. During the second half of July 1825, when he was working on *Boris Godunov,* he wrote on this topic to N. N. Raevsky: "Verisimilitude in the situations and truthfulness in the dialogue—that's the real rule of tragedy. I haven't read Calderón or Lope de Vega, but what a man that Shakespeare is! I can't get over it. How puny the 'tragic' Byron looks next to him. . . . Read Shakespeare, he's never afraid to compromise his characters, he lets them speak with all the range and spread of life, because he knows that he can give them their own individual language when the time and place calls for it."[8] In keeping with this concern for individual character and language, the speaking parts of *A Feast During the Plague* are so individualized that one could compose imaginary biographies for them: the "young man," no doubt a gentleman's son, one who has spent time at Oxford or Cambridge, who could quote Ben Jonson and discuss the latest play; Mary, the village girl who left home for the excitement and opportunities of the big city, only to be seduced and abandoned, and then to fall into the only way available for a woman with a damaged reputation to support herself; Louisa, the cynical prostitute, born into and thoroughly at home in the criminal underworld of London's slums, that now-lost world whose memory survives in *The Beggar's Opera* or Hogarth's paintings; the priest whose words, as they break into the revels, resound like thunder from the hills, like the unrecorded sermon of an unknown Jonathan Edwards; and finally Walsingham himself, now at once touched and condescending in his response to Mary's song, now using Louisa's fainting as the occasion to draw a philosophical lesson on human nature ("the cruel are weaker than the tender"), now proudly and fiercely defiant in his "Hymn to the Plague"—and beneath all of these facets, at last revealing himself as a despairing man trying to brave out a loss that he cannot accept.

This vividness of characterization can serve as a guide to the translator, by suggesting what type of language would be used by such a character if he or she were speaking not Russian but modern English. As an example, consider Louisa's speech:

Не в моде

Теперь такие песни! Но все же есть
Еще простые души: рады таять
От женских слез и слепо верят им.
Она уверена, что взор слезливый
Ее неотразим — а если б то же
О смехе думала своем, то верно,
Все б улыбалась. Вальсингам хвалил
Крикливых северных красавиц: вот
Она и расстоналась. Ненавижу
Волос шотландских этих желтизну.

When I went to translate the speech as a whole, it seemed to resist my efforts, but two specific details almost at once leapt into mind — "passé" for "не в моде" and "jaundice-yellow hair" for "волос . . . желтизну." The first of these two translations could be explained quite simply, as replacing a Gallicism in Russian, with its implicit claim to French sophistication, with a similar Gallicism in English. But where did the "jaundice-yellow hair" come from? It didn't seem to be merely a nonnative speaker's confusion of желтизна (yellowness, sallowness) with желтуха (jaundice); somehow it felt too strong, too convincingly right, particularly in view of the resistance I felt from all the other lines. After some thought, it came to me that the problem with translating this speech lay in its cynicism. Real thoroughgoing cynicism — as opposed to the sort that is a defense for a wounded sensitivity — is one of most difficult emotions to handle in poetry, because cynicism deadens the imagination while poetry heightens it. There is, however, a solution for this aesthetic problem in certain aspects of popular culture,

such as the hard-boiled detective novel or film noir: to use imagery
that conveys not only corruption but exaggerated corruption, so that
tedious emptiness is replaced by memorably jarring garishness. This
was what the "jaundice-yellow hair" was telling me: that the way to
give Louisa an English, or more exactly a 20th century American, voice
was to allow her to sound like a tough broad talking to a private eye:

> Now those songs
> Are hopelessly passé. But there are still
> Some fools who like to melt when women cry,
> Who'll swallow it hook, line, and sinker.
> She's decided that her tearful look
> Can't be resisted—if that's what she thought
> About her laugh, no doubt we'd see her
> Grinning all the time. Walsingham liked
> The weepy northern beauties—so of course
> She's got to moan and groan. I can't stand
> The jaundice-yellow hair of these Scotch girls.

As this example reminds us, just as the translator must always bear in
mind the characteristics of the language from which the work is being
translated—its history, its literature, its registers of vocabulary and
style—the translator must bear in mind the same characteristics for the
language into which the work is being translated. A target language
is not a linguistic blank slate. If the translator knows the literature of
the target language well and is skillful in evoking its associations, the
reader of the translation is more likely to perceive the work as "natural," graceful, and inevitable, rather than being distracted by devices
which, although fitting and acceptable in the original language, are not
in the spirit of the target language. A particularly interesting challenge
of this type occurs when translating the two songs in *A Feast During the Plague,* where it is necessary to make the songs believable as

English poems, which means that the reader or listener has to perceive them as fitting within the history and traditions of English poetry.

Since Mary's song is described by Walsingham as a Scottish folk song, it was to the Border ballads that I turned as a possible model for how her song might sound in English.[9] The subject of Mary's song is not a typical one for a ballad; but the terrible images of its second and third stanzas are no grimmer than "The Twa Corbies," and the promised constancy of Jenny no greater than that of "The Nut-Brown Maid." In terms of metrics, however, there is an important difference: a traditional English ballad is significantly less tightly structured than the Russian version of Mary's song. The stanzas of Pushkin's text have the rhyme scheme *abab;* by contrast, a ballad typically has the rhyme scheme *abcb.* The meter of Pushkin's text is trochaic tetrameter, with a perfectly regular alternation between eight-syllable and seven-syllable lines (the last unaccented syllable dropped). Both iambic and trochaic tetrameter are normal English ballad meters, but there are often slight metrical imperfections in some verses, which a singer no doubt compensated for by either doubling or omitting a note as the need arose. In terms of both rhyme scheme and meter, my translation adhered to the less formal poetics of the English ballad.

But as a draft English version emerged, I became more and more aware of a pronounced difference between Mary's song and the traditional ballad. The old ballads, with their stories of violent feuds and illicit love, were in a sense the tabloids of their day. When their narrative reaches a highly dramatic point, they sustain the terror as long as possible: think how many stanzas it takes before Sir Patrick Spens's doomed ship actually sinks, or before the condemned Young Waters actually reaches the gallows. A ballad-maker, presented with the material of Mary's song, would be unable to resist describing Jenny's deathbed agony, the lamentations of her family, Edmund's collapsing from grief at her funeral—all of which would so strongly emphasize the sufferings of the separated lovers as to overshadow what should be the climax of the song, its final two lines: "And Jenny will be true to Edmund / E'en in her place among the blest!" A ballad-maker, like a Baroque artist, reveled in the details with relatively little concern about how each part fitted into or affected the whole. The creator of Jenny's song, by contrast, subordinates the details to the overall artistic effect. Thus, an English counterpart to Mary's song would have to be thought of as the work of some minor poet who, while respecting the old tradition of popular song, nevertheless was producing a consciously shaped and edited imitation of it. This suggestion of literary affection for the traditional country way of thought and life led me to the "sentimentalist" poets, to Goldsmith and Cowper and Gray; and accordingly, although the rhythmic structure of my translation of Mary's song is that of a ballad, the vocabulary chosen was intended to evoke, not folk speech, but the style of language used in the poems of the pre-Romantics. At best, I hoped that my translation might call to mind a distant, less philosophical cousin of Gray's "Elegy in a Country Churchyard"; at least, that it would have a recognizable affinity with the relatively late and more literarily self-conscious ballads, such as "Barbara Allen" or "The Bailiff's Daughter of Islington."

Forming an idea of what Walsingham's song might have been like in English was less difficult. The song, in Russian, consists of six-line stanzas with a rhyme scheme *aabcbc*. In Russian, as in English, a six-line stanza is much less common than a four-line one. The relative rarity of this type of stanza suggested a deliberate choice on Pushkin's part, one that I felt could and should be observed also in translation. As for meter, the Russian version is in iambic tetrameter, a meter that is also common in English and transfers easily to it. In keeping with the poem's nature as a ringing rhetorical pronouncement, in the original version a pause could logically occur (or a singer take a breath) at the end of any line in a stanza, and there only; there are no enjambments. I tried to preserve the resulting syntax, with its terseness and forcefulness, as much as possible. Beyond that, to get some idea of what a poem like Walsingham's might have been like in English, I turned to those poets who celebrated a somewhat similar theme, the glory of warfare and danger. This led me to such now-forgotten later eighteenth-century poems as William Smyth's "The Soldier":

> Then, soldier! come fill high the wine,
> For we reck not of tomorrow;
> Be ours today and we resign
> All the rest to the fools of sorrow.
> Gay be the hour till we beat to arms —
> Then, comrade, Death or Glory;
> 'Tis Victory in all her charms,
> Or 'tis Fame in the world's bright story

or Thomas Osbert Mordaunt's

> Sound, sound the clarion, fill the fife!
>   Throughout the sensual world proclaim,
> One crowded hour of glorious life
>   Is worth an age without a name.

Such lyrics have a characteristic vocabulary that combines the simple and straightforward with obviously literary phrases ("we reck not," "sound the clarion"); I have tried to give Walsingham's this same style of language. And if the result turns out to be less satisfactory than I hoped, I can always take refuge in the fact that it was, after all, an amateur's effort — the first poem Walsingham ever wrote.

The use of a flexible rather than strict meter, which allows Pushkin's lines to be translated in a manner reflecting the cadences of contemporary English and thus gives the speeches of his characters emotional verisimilitude; the choice of an English vocabulary and style of expression for each character which is suited to that character's background and psychology; and the use of appropriate parts of the English literary tradition as a suggestive starting point for developing such a character-fitting style of expression — these are the principles that I have relied upon in my approach to translating the "little tragedies." These principles grew directly out of my own experience in reading the "little tragedies" in the original Russian: time and again I felt that I could perceive the characters themselves — the tones of their voices, their facial expressions, their gestures — and irresistibly I felt the desire to try to express that perception in English. The work resulting from this impulse is thus an interpretation of the "little tragedies" — interpretation not merely in the sense of a translation from one language to another, but also in the sense in which an actor interprets a role. It represents my understanding of, and tribute to, a masterpiece whose depths can long be explored, but never exhausted.

The Little Tragedies

The Miserly Knight

(Scenes from Chenstone's tragicomedy *The Covetous Knight*)

SCENE I

Albert: No matter what it costs, I shall appear
At the tournament. Show me my helmet, John.
(*John gives him the helmet.*)
It's pierced through, spoiled. It can't possibly
Be repaired. I'll have to get a new one.
What a hit! That damned Count Delorge!

John: And you paid him back and then some:
When you knocked him from his saddle,
He lay a whole day as if dead — and probably
Hasn't recovered yet.

Albert: Still, he lost nothing by it;
10   His breastplate of Venetian steel is whole,
                And his chest's his own; it costs him nothing;
                He won't be buying himself another.
                Why didn't I strip him of his helmet then!
                I would have, too, if I hadn't been ashamed
                In front of ladies and the Duke. Damned Count!
                Better if he had pierced my head.
                And I need clothes as well. Last time
                When all the knights wore satin and velvet,
                I alone of all at the Duke's table
20   Wore a coat-of-mail. I excused myself then
                By saying I'd just happened on the tourney.
                But what will I say now? Oh, this poverty!
                How vile, how it degrades one's heart!
                When Delorge with his heavy lance
                Pierced my helm and galloped on past,
                And I bareheaded turned and spurred
                My Emir, flew like a whirlwind
                And flung the count some twenty paces
                Like a page boy; when all the ladies
30   Rose from their seats, when Clotild herself,
                Who'd covered her eyes, couldn't help but shout,
                And the heralds paid honor to my blow—
                No one then thought about the reason
                For my valor and my wondrous strength!
                I was seized by fury at my damaged helmet,
                What's to blame for my heroism? —miserliness.
                Pah! It's not difficult to catch it here
                Under the same roof as my father.
                How's my poor Emir?

John:	Still limping; You can't ride him for some time yet.
Albert:	There's nothing for it, then: I'll buy the bay. They're not asking much for him.
John:	Not much, but we don't have the money.
Albert:	What's that good-for-nothing Solomon say?
John:	He says that he can't loan you Any more money without collateral.
Albert:	Collateral! where'd I get collateral, the devil!
John:	That's what I told him.
Albert:	What'd he say?
John:	Groaned and waffled.
Albert:	Then you should've told him my father's Rich as a Jew himself, and sooner or later I'll inherit everything.
John:	That's what I said.
Albert:	What'd he say?
John:	Waffled and groaned.
Albert:	What a mess!
John:	He was going to come himself.
Albert:	Well, thank God. I won't let him out without a ransom.

(*Knock at the door.*)

Who's there?

(*The Jew enters.*)

Jew: Your humble servant.

Albert: Ah, friend!
You damned Jew, honorable Solomon,
Come over here; so—you, I hear,
Don't believe in credit.

Jew: Ah, merciful knight,
I swear to you: I'd be glad . . . truly, I can't.
Where would I get money? I've ruined myself
Through my zeal for always helping knights.
No one repays. I wanted to ask you
If you couldn't give me even just part . . .

Albert: Robber!
If I had any money, would I be
Fooling around with you? Enough,
Don't be stubborn, my dear Solomon;
Give me some gold. Send me a hundred pieces
Before I have you searched.

Jew: A hundred!
If only I had a hundred gold pieces!

Albert: Listen:
Aren't you ashamed not to help
Your friends?

Jew: I swear to you . . .

Albert: Enough, enough.
You demand collateral? what rubbish!
What collateral should I give you?—a pig's skin?
If I had anything I could offer, long ago

I'd have sold it. Or is the word of a knight
Worth so little to you, you dog?

Jew: Your word,
So long as you shall live, is worth a great deal.
All the treasure chests of Flemish merchants
It will open like a magic wand.

80   But when it's given to me, a lowly Jew,
And should—God forbid—you die, then
In my hands it will be of no more value
Than the key to a casket flung into the ocean.

Albert: Can my father possibly outlive me?

Jew: Who knows? Our days are numbered by Another;
Last night a youth was healthy, now he's dead
And there you see four gray-haired men
Carrying his coffin on their stooped shoulders.
The Baron's in good health. God willing, ten years, twenty,

90   Even twenty-five or thirty he could live.

Albert: You're lying, Jew; besides, in thirty years,
I'll be pushing fifty, and then what use
Will I have for the money?

Jew: Money? — Money
Is always, whatever our age, useful to us;
But a young man sees it as a servant
And doesn't hesitate to send it far and wide.
An old man sees it as a trusty friend
And guards it as the apple of his eye.

Albert: Oh, for my father money's not a servant

100   Or a friend, but a master; he himself serves it.
And serves it—how? like an Algerian slave,
Like a dog on a chain. A kennel with no heat

Is his home, he drinks water, eats dry crusts,
He never sleeps at night, just runs and barks.
And the gold lies there resting peacefully
In the chests. Enough! Some day
It'll serve me and forget what resting is.

Jew: Yes, at the Baron's funeral
            More money than tears will be poured forth.
110   May God send you your inheritance soon!

Albert: Amen!

Jew: But perhaps . . .

Albert: What?

Jew: It occurred to me there is
            A certain means . . .

Albert: What means?

Jew: This:
            There is an old man whom I know,
            A Jew, a poor apothecary . . .

Albert: A usurer
            Like yourself, or even a bit more honest?

Jew: No, sir, Tobias has a different trade —
            He mixes drops — it's really amazing
            What an effect they have.

Albert: Well, so?

Jew: They go in a glass of water — three drops will do,
120   There's no taste, no color, nothing you'd notice;
            A man won't suffer any indigestion
            Or nausea, or any pain — but he'll die.

Albert: Your old man deals in poison.

Jew: Yes,
Poison too.

Albert: And so? Instead of loaning money,
You're offering me two hundred vials of poison,
At one gold piece per vial. Is that it?

Jew: You're pleased to have your joke at my expense —
No; I meant . . . perhaps you . . . well, I thought
The Baron's time had come to die.

130 Albert: What! Poison my father! You dare face a son . . .
John! Seize him. You dare say this to me! . . .
Get this straight, you Jewish heart,
You dog, you snake, I'll have you hanged
This instant at the castle gate.

Jew: I'm guilty!
Have mercy: I was joking.

Albert: John, bring a rope.

Jew: I . . . I was joking. I've brought you money.

Albert: Out, dog!

(*The Jew leaves.*)

                This is what my father's miserliness
Has brought me to! To have a Jew dare
Propose that to me! Bring me a glass of wine,
140 I'm shaking like a leaf. . . . But I still need money.
John, go catch up with that damned Jew
And take his gold. And bring the inkwell here.
I'll give him a receipt, the crook — but don't
Bring that Judas in here. . . . No, wait.

His gold pieces will stink of poison,
Like his kinsman's silver did. . . .
I asked for wine.

John: We don't have any wine,
            Not a drop.

Albert: What about the gift
            That Raymond sent me from Spain?

150   John: Yesterday I took the last bottle
            To the sick blacksmith.

Albert: Yes, I remember, I know. . . .
            Give me water then. What a damned life!
            No, it's settled—I'll go and seek my rights
            From the Duke; let him make my father
            Support me like his son, not like some mouse
            Born under a floorboard.

SCENE II

Baron: Like a young skirt-chaser who waits for when
            He'll meet his bimbo—some tramp on the make,
            Or some fool he's snowed—that's how all day
160   I wait for the minute I go down
            Into my secret vault, to the faithful chests.
            Today's a happy day! Now I can open
            The sixth chest (the one that's not full yet)
            And pour in a handful of piled-up gold.
            Not much, it seems, but little by little
            The treasure grows. Once I read
            About a king who ordered his men
            To bring, each one, a handful of earth,

And a mighty hill rose up — and the king
Could gaze down merrily from that height
Upon the valleys, covered with white tents,
And on the sea, where ships were sailing.
Thus I, bringing my poor handfuls one by one,
Bearing my accustomed tribute to my vault,
Have built up my hill — and from its height
I can gaze on all that's in my power.
What's not in my power? From here,
Like a demon I can rule the world.
If I just want it — palaces will spring up;
Into my splendid gardens there will dance
A company of playful nymphs;
The Muses too will bring me tribute,
Free genius will become my slave,
And virtue and unsleeping toil
Will meekly look to me for their reward.
Just let me whistle — bloodstained villainy
Obediently and timidly will crawl to me
And lick my hand, and peer into my eyes,
Looking for a sign of my will there.
To me all things submit, and I — to none;
I stand above desire; I am calm;
I know my might; this knowledge
Is enough for me. . . .

(*Looks at his gold.*)

It seems like little enough,
But how much human care and woe,
How many lies, tears, prayers, and curses
It stands for — what a heavy load!
There's one old doubloon — right here. Now
The widow's given it to me, but first

She knelt with her three children at my window
200 For half a day, howling all the time.
It rained, and stopped, and started again,
The faker, she didn't budge; I could, of course,
Have chased her off, but something told me
That she'd brought me what her husband owed,
And wouldn't want to find herself in jail next day.
And this one? — I got this one from Thibault —
Where'd he get it from, the lazy cheat?
Stole it, most likely; or, who knows,
On the highway, in the woods, at night. . . .
210 If all the blood, sweat, and tears once shed
For all that's stored in here, could now pour forth
From the earth's bowels in one sudden gush,
There'd be a second Flood — and I would suffocate
Inside my faithful vault. But enough.

(*He goes to open the chest.*)

Every single time, when I start to open
A chest, I feel feverish and tremble.
Not from fear (no! what should I fear?
I have my sword; my tempered blade
Will answer for the gold), but from some sense,
220 Mysterious and dread, which grips my heart. . . .
Doctors assure us that there are people
Who find pleasure in committing murder.
When I put the key into the lock, then
I feel what such a one must feel, plunging
His knife into a victim: pleasure
And horror mixed in one.

(*Opens the chest.*)

My bliss!

(*Drops the coins in.*)

There, now you've roamed enough throughout the world,
Serving the passions and needs of men,
Sleep now, the sleep of strength and peace,
230   As the gods sleep in far-off heavens. . . .
Today I want to give myself a feast:
I'll light a candle in front of each chest
And open all of them, and I'll stand
Amid them all, looking at the glittering piles.

(*He lights candles and opens the chests one after another.*)

I am a king! . . . What an enchanting glitter!
Obeying me, my realm indeed is mighty;
It holds my joy, my honor, and my glory!
I am a king . . . but who will follow me,
Who will take this power? My heir!

240 A boy who throws money around like mad,
 With his hellraising friends out for a good time!
 No sooner than I've died, he! He'll come here
 Into these peaceful and long-silent vaults,
 With a pack of greedy courtiers at his heels.
 After stealing the keys from my dead body,
 He'll laugh as he throws open all the chests.
 And all my treasures will flow out
 And pour through the holes of satin pockets.
 He'll break into bits the sacred vessels,
250 Let dirt drink up the coronation oil —
 He'll squander it. . . . And by what right?
 Have I really acquired all this for nothing,
 Or just for play, as if I were a gambler
 Rolling the dice and and raking in my piles?
 Who knows how much bitter self-restraint,
 What passions choked back, what weary thoughts,
 What cares day after day, what sleepless nights
 All this cost me? Or will my son say
 That my heart's long overgrown with moss,
260 That I feel no desire, that even my conscience
 Never gnawed at me, my conscience,
 That beast with claws that tear my heart — my conscience,
 That guest I didn't invite, a wearying companion,
 That harsh demanding creditor, that witch
 Who makes the moon hide and who troubles graves,
 Making them give up their dead? . . .
 No, first suffer through piling up your own wealth,
 And then let's see if some unhappy man
 Will come and squander what you got by blood.
270 Oh, if only I could hide this vault from all
 Unworthy eyes! Oh, if from my grave

I could arise, a ghostly watchman,
And sit upon the chest, and guard my treasures
Against the living, as I guard them now!

SCENE III

(*In the palace.*)

Albert: Believe me, my lord, I have long borne
The shame of bitter poverty. Were my need not great,
You would not have heard my complaint.

Duke: I do believe you; a noble knight
Such as yourself, would not accuse his father
Unless his need was great. Few men are so corrupt . . .
Don't fear; I'll urge your father to act honorably,
But I'll do it in private, without scandal.
I expect him soon. It's a long time since I've seen him.
He and my grandfather were friends. I remember,
When I was just a boy still, how
He'd lift me up and seat me on his steed
And put his heavy helmet on me — it covered me
As if it were a church bell.

(*Looks out the window.*)

                          Who's that?
Is it he?

Albert: Yes, my lord.

Duke: Wait
In that chamber. I will call you.

(*Albert exits; enter the Baron.*)

Baron,
I am glad to see you well and in good spirits.

Baron: I am happy, my lord, that I had the strength
To come into your presence at your command.

Duke: You've been away a long time, baron,
A long time. Do you remember me?

Baron: I, my lord?
I see you as if it were now. Oh, you were
A boy with spirit. The late duke
Used to say to me: Philip (he always called
Me Philip), what do you think? Eh?
300   Twenty years from now, for sure, the two of us,
We'll be nothing compared to that kid . . .
To you, that is . . .

Duke: We'll now renew
Our acquaintance. You have forgotten my court.

Baron: I'm an old man now, my lord; what should
I do at court? You're young, you love
Tournaments and fêtes. But for such things I
Am no longed suited. If God sends war, then I
Am ready to climb wheezing onto my horse;
I'll still find strength enough to draw
310   My old sword for you with a trembling arm.

Duke: Baron, your devotion is well known to us;
You were my grandfather's friend; my father
Esteemed you. And I have always considered you
A loyal and brave knight—but let's sit down.
Baron, do you have any children?

Baron: One son.

Duke:	Why don't I see him near me?
	You're weary of the court, but it would befit him,
	At his age and with his rank, to be near me.

Baron:	My son dislikes a noisy fashionable life;
320	He's unsociable and gloomy by nature —
	All day he wanders the forests round the castle
	Like a young deer.

Duke:	It's not good for him
	To be so unsociable. We'll soon teach him
	About gaiety, about balls and tournaments.
	Send him to me; provide your son
	With an estate fitting to his rank . . .
	You're frowning, are you weary from the road,
	Perhaps?

Baron:	My Lord, I am not weary,
	But you've embarrassed me. I would rather
330	Not have admitted it to you, but you
	Have forced me to say about my son
	Something I wanted to hide from you.
	He, my Lord, unhappily is not worthy
	Of either your favor or your attention.
	He's spending his youth in rowdiness,
	Engaging in low vices . . .

Duke:	That, Baron,
	Is because he's alone. Solitude
	And idleness destroy young people.
	Send him to us: he'll forget
340	Habits that arose up-country.

| Baron: | Forgive me, but, truly, my lord, |
| | I cannot consent to that . . . |

Duke:	Why then?
Baron:	Spare an old man . . .
Duke:	I command: tell me the reason For your refusal.
Baron:	I'm angered at My son.
Duke:	Why?
Baron:	For his wicked crime.
Duke:	And what, tell me, was that?
Baron:	Spare me, Duke . . .
Duke:	This is very strange, Or are you ashamed of him?
Baron:	Yes . . . ashamed . . .
Duke:	But what did he do?
Baron:	He . . . he meant To murder me.
Duke:	Murder! I'll hand him over To justice as a foul villain.
Baron:	I won't set out to prove it, but I know That my death is what he's thirsting for, And I know that he's made an attempt At . . .
Duke:	What?
Baron:	Robbing me.

(Albert bursts into the room.)

Albert:	Baron, you're lying.
Duke:	(*To the son.*)
	How dare you? . . .
Baron:	You're here! You dare face me! . . .
	You can say a thing like that to your father! . . .
	I'm lying! And in the presence of our lord! . . .

360

	To me . . . or am I no longer a knight?
Albert:	You're a liar.
Baron:	And lightning hasn't struck him, righteous God!
	Then take this, and let the sword judge between us!

(*He flings his gauntlet, his son hastily picks it up.*)

Albert:	My thanks. Here's my first gift from my father.
Duke:	What did I see? What's this — and in my presence?
	A son accepted the challenge of his old father!
	In what times have I taken upon myself
	The ducal chain! Silence: You, madman,
	And you, tiger cub! Enough.

(*To the son.*)

	Give it up;
	Hand me that gauntlet.

(*He takes it.*)

Albert:	(*Aside.*)
	A pity.

370

Duke:	How he plunged his claws into it! — the monster!
	Go: do not dare appear in my presence
	Until that time when I myself
	Shall send for you.

(*Albert exits.*)

You, unhappy old man,

Are you not ashamed . . .

Baron: Forgive me, my lord,
I cannot stand . . . My knees are giving way . . .
It's stifling! . . . Stifling! . . . Where are the keys?
My keys, keys! . . .

Duke: He's dead. God!
A terrible age, terrible hearts!

Mozart and Salieri

(*A room.*)

Salieri: They say there's no justice here on earth,
But there's no justice higher up, either. To me
That's as clear and simple as do-re-mi.
I was born with a love for art;
When I was a child, when up on high
The organ's notes echoed in our old church,
I listened and was spellbound — I wept,
Sweet tears flowed against my will.

Early I refused all idle amusements;
To know anything other than music was
Hateful to me; stubbornly and proudly
I denied all else and gave myself up
To music alone. The first steps were hard
And the first path was tedious. I overcame
My early difficulties. I gave craft
Its place as the foundation stone of art;
I made myself a craftsman; my fingers
Acquired obedient, cold dexterity
And my ear, accuracy. I killed sounds,
Dissected music like a corpse. I put harmony
To the test of algebra. Only after that,
Experienced in my studies, did I dare
Allow myself the luxury of creative dreams.
I began creating; but silently, in secret,
Not daring even to think yet of glory.
Often, after sitting silently in my cell
Two or three days, forgetting sleep and food,
After the taste of ecstasy and tears of inspiration,
I burned my work and watched coldly
As my idea and the sounds I had brought forth
Blazed up, then vanished with a puff of smoke.
What am I saying? When the great Gluck
Appeared and revealed to us new mysteries
(Deep and captivating mysteries),
Didn't I abandon everything I'd known before,
Everything I'd loved and believed so fervently,
And didn't I set out boldly after him
Without a murmur, like one who's lost his path
And is directed to go another way?
By concentrated, constant effort
Finally in the unbounded realm of art

I achieved a high place. Glory
Smiled on me; in people's hearts
I found the harmonies that I'd created.
I was happy: I peacefully enjoyed
My work, success, renown; as well as
The works and the successes of my friends,
My colleagues in the miracles of art.
No! I never once felt envy then,

50   No, never!—not even when Piccini
Learned to charm the savage Paris audience,
Not even when I heard for the first time
The opening chords of *Iphigenia*.
Who will say that proud Salieri
Was ever a contemptible envier,
A snake trodden powerless underfoot,
Left half-alive to bite the dirt and dust?
No one! . . . But now—I say it myself—now
I am an envier. I feel envy; deep,

60   Tormenting envy. Oh heaven!
Where is rightness, when the sacred gift,
Immortal genius, comes not as reward
For ardent love and self-renunciation,
Labor, zeal, diligence, and prayers—
But bestows its radiant halo on a madman
Who idly strolls through life? Oh, Mozart, Mozart!

Mozart: Aha! You saw me! And I wanted
To give you a surprise amusement.

Salieri: You're here!—When'd you get here?

Mozart: Just now.

70   I was walking here, coming to show you something,
And as I went by a tavern, suddenly

I heard a fiddle. . . . No, my friend Salieri,
You've never heard anything funnier
In all your life. . . . This blind fiddler in the tavern
Was sawing away at "Voi che sapete." Splendid!
I couldn't resist, I brought the fiddler here
So I could treat you to his art.
Come in!

(*An old blind man with a violin enters.*)

Play some Mozart for us!

(*The fiddler plays an aria from* Don Giovanni;
Mozart laughs.)

Salieri: And you can laugh?

Mozart: Oh, Salieri!
80   Really you don't laugh at that?

Salieri: No.
I don't find it funny when some worthless dauber
Makes smears and drips on Raphael's Madonna,
I don't find it funny when some vulgar showman
Reels off a parody that dishonors Dante.
Be off, old man.

Mozart: Wait: here's something for you,
Drink to my health.

(*The old man exits.*)

                  Right now, Salieri,
You're not in a good mood. I'll come see you
Another time.

Salieri: What'd you bring me?

Mozart: Oh, nothing—just a trifle. Late last night
90   My insomnia tormented me,
            And two or three ideas crossed my mind.
            Today I sketched them out. I wanted
            To find out what you thought; but right now
            You don't feel like hearing me.

Salieri: Oh, Mozart, Mozart!
            When don't I feel like hearing you? Sit down;
            I'm listening.

Mozart: (*At the piano.*)
                              Imagine someone—who?
            Well, say myself—only a little younger;
            In love—not all that deeply, but a little—
            I'm with a pretty girl, or with a friend—say you,
100   I'm in good spirits—Just then, a ghostly vision,
            A sudden gloom, or something of that sort . . .
            Well, listen.

            (*He plays.*)

Salieri: You were coming to me with that
            And you could stop off at a tavern
            And listen to a blind fiddler!—My God!
            Mozart, you're not worthy of yourself.

Mozart: What, it's good?

Salieri: What depth!
            What boldness and what just proportion!
            You, Mozart, are a god, and you yourself don't know it;
            I know it, I know.

Mozart: Bah! really? well, maybe . . .
110   But my divineness is hungry.

Salieri: Listen: let's have dinner together
                At the Sign of the Golden Lion.

Mozart: If you want;
                I'd be glad to. Let me run home first
                To tell my wife she shouldn't wait for me
                For dinner.

(*He exits.*)

Salieri: I'll be expecting you, remember!
                No! I cannot set myself against
                My destiny—I am the one who's chosen
                To stop him—or else we all will perish,
                All of us, priests and servitors of music,
120   Not only I with my empty glory . . .
                What is the use if Mozart lives
                And even achieves still greater heights?
                What he does—will he elevate Art? No,
                It will fall again when he has vanished;
                No heir of his will remain among us.
                What use is he? Appearing like an angel,
                He brings us a few of Heaven's songs,
                And then, once he's roused a wingless desire
                In us, children of dust, he flies away!
130   Fly away then! And the sooner, the better!

                Here is the poison, my Izora's final gift.
                For eighteen years I've carried it with me—
                And often in that time I have found life
                An unbearable wound, and often I have sat
                At table with a heedless enemy,
                And, yes, I heard the whisper of temptation
                But I didn't yield, although I am no coward,
                Although I feel an injury deeply,

Although I love life little. Still I waited.
When the thirst for death tormented me,
Why die? — I thought: it may be, life
Will bring me unexpected gifts;
Rapture, it may be, will come to me
In a creative night of inspiration;
It may be some new Haydn will bring forth
Greatness — and I will rejoice in it . . .
When I feasted with a hated guest,
It may be — I thought — a still worse foe
Awaits me; an injury still worse, it may be,
Will strike me down from some proud height —
Then you won't be in vain, Izora's gift.
And I was right! At last I've found
My enemy, and at last a new Haydn
Wondrously has enraptured me!
Now it's time! cherished gift of love,
For you to go today into friendship's cup.

SCENE II

(*A private room in a tavern; a piano.
Mozart and Salieri are at the table.*)

Salieri: Why are you gloomy today?

Mozart: Me? Not at all!

Salieri: Surely, Mozart, something has upset you?
The food is good, the wine is splendid,
And you sit silently and frown.

Mozart: I must admit,
My *Requiem* is troubling me.

Salieri:	Ah!
	You've been working on a requiem? For long?

Mozart: Yes, long, about three weeks. But a strange thing . . .
            Haven't I told you?

Salieri: No.

Mozart: Then listen.
            Three weeks ago, one night I came home
            Late. They told me somebody'd come by
            And asked for me. Why—I don't know,
            But all night I thought: who could it be?
            And what was I to him? The next day
170   The same man came and didn't find me in.
            The day after I was playing on the floor
            With my little boy. Someone called me;
            I went out. A man dressed all in black
            Greeted me respectfully, ordered from me
            A requiem, and vanished. I sat down
            And began to write at once—and since then
            My black man's never come back to my house;
            And I'm glad; I'd hate to have to part
            With my work, although the *Requiem*
180   Already is complete. But meanwhile I . . .

Salieri: What?

Mozart: I'm embarrassed to admit this . . .

Salieri: What?

Mozart: Day and night my black man won't
            Leave me alone. Everywhere I go
            He follows like a shadow. Even now,

It seems to me, he's sitting with us
As a third.

Salieri: Rubbish! What childish fear is this?
Drop this useless brooding. Beaumarchais
Used to tell me, "Brother Salieri, listen:
When black thoughts come to trouble you,
190   Pop the cork on a bottle of champagne,
Or reread *The Marriage of Figaro*."

Mozart: Good! Beaumarchais was after all your friend;
You wrote the music for his *Tarara*,
A splendid thing. There's a motif in it . . .
I'm always singing it when I am happy . . .
La la la la. . . . Ah, is it true, Salieri,
That Beaumarchais poisoned someone?

Salieri: I don't think so; he was too much a buffoon
For such a craft.

Mozart: He's a genius,
200   Like you and me. And genius and crime
Are two things that don't combine. Isn't that true?

Salieri: You think so?

(Pours the poison into Mozart's glass.)

               Well then, drink.

Mozart: To your
Health, my friend, and to the faithful union
That binds together Mozart and Salieri,
Two sons of harmony.

(He drinks.)

| Salieri: | Stop, |
| | Stop, stop! . . . You drank it . . . without me? |

| Mozart: | (*Tosses his napkin on the table.*) |
| | I've had enough. |

(*Goes to the piano.*)

Salieri, listen to
My *Requiem*.

(*He plays.*)

You're weeping?

Salieri: These tears
Are the first I've shed—from pain and pleasure,
As if I had fulfilled a burdening duty,
As if the surgeon's knife had cut from me
The part that suffered! Friend Mozart, these tears . . .
Don't notice them. Continue, still make haste
To fill my soul with sounds . . .

Mozart: If only everyone could feel the power
Of harmony like you! but no, for then
The world could not exist; no one would want
To spend time taking care of life's low needs;
All would be given over to free art.
We are but few, we chosen, happy idlers
Who look disdainfully at petty usefulness
And form a priesthood serving only beauty.
Isn't that so? But now I feel unwell.
Something weighs me down; I want to sleep.
Farewell!

Salieri: Until we meet again.

(*Alone.*)

You will sleep

A long time, Mozart! But is he really right
And am I not a genius? Genius and crime
Are two things that don't combine. That's not true:
What of Michelangelo? or is that just a fable
230   Of the stupid, senseless crowd — and it was not
A murderer who designed the Vatican?

The Stone Guest

Leporello: O statua gentilissima
         Del gran' Commendatore! . . .
         . . . Ah, Padrone!

Don Giovanni

SCENE I

Don Juan: We'll wait for nightfall here. At long last
               We've reached the walls of Madrid! Soon
               I'll be dashing through the well-known streets,
               My cape covering my chin and my hat, my eyes.
               What do you think? Could I be recognized?

Leporello: Oh yeah, it's tough to recognize Don Juan!
               There's a swarm of men like him!

Don Juan: Are you kidding?
               Who's going to recognize me?

Leporello: The first watchman,
Some gypsy girl or drunken street-musician,
10   Or one of your own kind, some swaggering lord
With a sword at his side and wearing a cape.

Don Juan: So what if they do know me — so long as
I don't meet the king himself. But still,
I'm not afraid of anyone in Madrid.

Leporello: And tomorrow word will reach the king
That Don Juan violated his exile
And showed up in Madrid — what do you think
He'll do to you then?

Don Juan: Send me back.
He's hardly going to cut off my head.
20   After all, I'm not a state criminal.
He sent me away although he loves me,
To keep me out of reach of the family
Of the man I killed . . .

Leporello: That's just it!
You should have stayed there — out of reach.

Don Juan: Your humble servant! I was on the point
Of dying of boredom there. What people,
What a country! Even the sky's just smoke.
And the women? Let me tell you something,
My foolish Leporello: I wouldn't trade
30   The lowliest peasant girl there is in Andalusia
For the foremost of their beauties — that's the truth.
Oh, at first I was intrigued by them —
By their blue eyes and their fair complexions,
Their modesty, and most of all, their novelty;
But, thank God, soon I saw through them —

It's a sin to even flirt with women such as that—
They're not alive, they're nothing but wax dolls;
But our women! . . . Wait a minute, we know
This place already; do you recall it?

40 Leporello: How could I not know it: yes, I remember
The Monastery of St. Anthony. We'd ride here
And I'd hold the horses over there in the grove.
A damned bad job, let me tell you. You
Spent your time here a lot more pleasantly
Than I did, believe me.

Don Juan: (*Pensively*)
                              Poor Inez!
She's gone now! how I loved her!

Leporello: Inez!—the black-eyed one. . . . Now I remember,
For three months you were paying court
To her; it was all the devil could do to help.

50 Don Juan: July it was . . . at night. I found strange pleasure
In gazing at her sorrowful eyes
And death-pale lips. It's strange.
You apparently didn't think she was
A beauty. And in fact, there wasn't
Much beautiful about her. Her eyes,
Just her eyes. And her glance . . . I've never seen
Another glance like that. And her voice
Was quiet, feeble—like a sick woman's—
Her husband was a worthless wretch, and stern—
60 I found that out too late—Poor Inez! . . .

Leporello: Well, so, after her came others.

Don Juan: True.

Leporello:	And while we're still alive, there'll be still more.
Don Juan:	Also true.
Leporello:	So what woman in Madrid Are we going to go after?
Don Juan:	Oh, Laura! I'll head straight for her house.
Leporello:	That's it.
Don Juan:	I'll walk right through her door — and if there's company, I'll invite him to make his exit through the window.
Leporello:	Of course. And now we've cheered right up. Dead women don't trouble us for long. Who's that coming toward us?

(A monk enters.)

Monk:	She's coming Now. Who's this? Are you Doña Anna's people?
Leporello:	No, we're gentlemen, our own masters, Out strolling here.
Don Juan:	Whom are you expecting?
Monk:	Doña Anna should be coming to visit Her husband's grave.
Don Juan:	Doña Anna De Solva! The wife of the knight-commander Killed by . . . I forgot his name?
Monk:	The shameless, Godless profligate, Don Juan.

Leporello:		What do you think of that? Don Juan's fame
80		Has penetrated even a peaceful monastery,
		The anchorites sing his praises.

Monk: You know him, perhaps?

Leporello: Us? Not at all.
So where's he now?

Monk: No longer here,
He's in exile far away.

Leporello: Thank God.
The farther, the better. Would all such profligates
Were sewn up in a sack and thrown into the sea!

Don Juan: What nonsense are you talking?

Leporello: Quiet: it's on purpose . . .

Don Juan: So this is where the knight-commander's buried?

Monk:		Yes; his wife set up a monument for him,
90		And every day without fail she comes here
		To say prayers for the soul of the departed
		And to weep.

Don Juan: What strange kind of widow's this?
And not bad-looking?

Monk: We anchorites must not
Be tempted by the loveliness of women,
But lying is a sin; a saint himself could not
Look unmoved upon her wondrous beauty.

Don Juan: There's the reason her husband was so jealous.
Doña Anna always was kept locked up inside,

100	None of us have ever so much as seen her. Would that I could speak with her.

Monk: Oh, Doña Anna never says a word
To a man.

Don Juan: Not even to you, Father?

Monk: That's different; I'm a monk.
There she is.

(*Doña Anna enters.*)

Doña Anna: Father, open the gate.

Monk: Coming, señora; I was expecting you.

(*Doña Anna follows the monk.*)

Leporello: So, what's she like?

Don Juan: You can't see anything
Under her black veil and widow's weeds.
I caught one glimpse of a narrow heel.

Leporello: For you, that's enough. Your imagination
110   Will fill in all the blank spots in a minute;
It works faster than a portrait painter
And you don't care what it begins with,
A forehead or a foot.

Don Juan: Listen, Leporello,
I'm going to meet her.

Leporello: That's just what we need!
What next! He's bumped off the husband
And now he wants to see the widow's tears.
Shameless!

Don Juan: But it's already gotten dark.
                     Before the moon can rise above our heads
                     And turn the darkness into shining dusk,
120   We'll go into Madrid.

Leporello: A Spanish grandee
                     Who waits for dark and fears the moon, like a thief—
                     God! Damn this life. How much longer
                     Will I have to drag after him? I'm worn out.

SCENE II

(*A room. Dinner at Laura's.*)

First Guest: I swear, Laura, that you've never acted
                     With such perfection as you did today.
                     How well you understood your character!

Second Guest: How powerfully you developed your role!

Third Guest: And with what art!

Laura: Yes, today every word,
                     Every gesture came out well for me.
130   I gave myself up freely to inspiration.
                     The words poured out as if they were brought forth,
                     Not by slavish memory, but by the heart . . .

First Guest: True.
                     Even now your eyes are shining yet,
                     Your cheeks still burn, the ecstasy
                     Has not gone from you. Laura, do not let
                     It cool and die in silence; sing, Laura,
                     Sing something.

Laura:	Give me my guitar.

(*She sings.*)

All:	Oh, brava! brava! Wonderful! Splendid!

First Guest: Our thanks, enchantress. With your spells
             You charm our hearts. Among life's pleasures
             Music yields to none save love;
             But love itself is melody . . . look:
             Even Carlos is moved, your gloomy guest.

Second Guest: What sounds! How much soul there is in them!
             Whose wrote the lyrics, Laura?

Laura:	Don Juan.

Don Carlos: What? Don Juan?

Laura: It was written by
             My faithful friend and fickle lover.

Don Carlos: Your Don Juan's a godless scoundrel,
             And you, you're a fool.

Laura: Have you gone mad?
             I'll have my servants cut your throat
             This minute, Spanish grandee or no.

Don Carlos: (*Rises.*)
             Call them then.

First Guest: Laura, stop;
             Don Carlos, don't get angry. She forgot . . .

Laura: What? That Juan killed his brother
             Honorably in a duel? True; it's a pity
             It wasn't him.

Don Carlos:	I'm foolish to get angry.
Laura:	Aha! You say yourself you're foolish. So let's make up.
Don Carlos:	It's my fault, Laura, Forgive me. But still you know: that name Is one I cannot hear indifferently . . .
Laura:	Is it my fault, that constantly That name keeps coming to my tongue?
Guest:	Well, to show that you're no longer angry, Laura, sing another song.
Laura:	Yes, as a farewell, It's time for you to go, it's night. What shall I sing? Ah, listen.

(*Sings.*)

All:	Delightful, splendid!
Laura:	Good night now, gentlemen.
Guests:	Good night, Laura.

(*They leave. Laura stops Don Carlos.*)

Laura:	You, madman! You stay here with me, You've caught my fancy; you reminded me Of Don Juan, the way you scolded me And clenched your teeth and gnashed them.
Don Carlos:	Lucky man! You loved him then.

(*Laura nods.*)

Very much?

160

170

Laura: Very much.

Don Carlos: Do you love him now?

Laura: This minute?
          No, I don't. I can't love two at once.
          Right now it's you I love.

Don Carlos: Tell me, Laura,
          How old are you?

Laura: Eighteen.

Don Carlos: You're young now . . . and you'll still be young
          For five or six more years. You'll draw
          The men around you six more years,
180   To pay you court and give you presents,
          To sing you serenades at night,
          And for your sake to kill each other
          In darkness at the crossroads. But when
          The time comes that your eyes have sunk,
          Their lids grown wrinkled and discolored,
          And your hair is streaked with gray,
          And men start calling you "old woman,"
          Then — what will you say?

Laura: Then? Why should
          I think of that? What talk is this?
190   Or do you always have such thoughts?
          Come to the balcony. How calm the sky is,
          The air is warm and still, the night is fragrant
          With scents of lime and laurel, the moon
          Shines radiant in the deep dark blue,
          And the watchman cries, "A-a-all's well!" . . .
          And far off, to the north — in Paris —

Perhaps the sky is gray with clouds,
Cold rain is falling, the wind howls.
But what is that to us? Look, Carlos,
I'm ordering you to smile . . .
There you go!

Don Carlos: Sweet demon!

(*A knock.*)

Don Juan: Hey! Laura!

Laura: Who's there? Whose voice is that?

Don Juan: Open up . . .

Laura: Can it be! . . . Oh God! . . .

(*She opens the door, Don Juan enters.*)

Don Juan: Good evening . . .

Laura: Don Juan!

(*Laura flings herself upon his neck.*)

Don Carlos: What! Don Juan! . . .

Don Juan: Laura, my love! . . .

(*He kisses her.*)

Who's here with you, my Laura?

Don Carlos: I,
            Don Carlos.

Don Juan: An unexpected meeting!
Tomorrow I'll be at your service.

Don Carlos: No!
                   Now—right now.

Laura: Don Carlos, stop it!
                   This isn't a public place—you're in my house—
210   Kindly leave.

Don Carlos: (*Not hearing her.*)
                              I'm waiting. Well, come on,
                   I see you've got your sword.

Don Juan: If you're
                   So impatient, as you wish.

                   (*They fight.*)

Laura: Oh! Oh! Juan!

                   (*She throw herself on the bed.*)

                   (*Don Carlos falls.*)

Don Juan: Get up, Laura, it's all over.

Laura: What's this?
                   Killed? That's great! And in my room!
                   So what do I do now, you shameless devil?
                   How do I get rid of him?

Don Juan: Maybe
                   He's still alive.

Laura: Yeah, right! Look, you damned fool,
                   You stuck him through the heart—straight through,
                   There's no blood coming out from a three-cornered wound,
220   And he's not breathing—what's that mean?

Don Juan: So
                   What could I do? He asked for it.

Laura: Eh, Don Juan,
          What a nuisance. Up to your old tricks,
          But never guilty. . . . Where did you come from?
          Have you been here long?

Don Juan: I just got here,
          And on the quiet—I'm not pardoned.

Laura: And straightaway you thought of Laura?
          All's well that ends well. That's enough,
          I don't believe it. You were passing by
          And chanced to see my house.

Don Juan: No, Laura,
230   Ask Leporello. I'm staying outside the city
          In a hellhole of an inn. It was my Laura
          I came to find in Madrid.

          (*He kisses her.*)

Laura: My love!
          Stop! . . . with the dead man there! . . . what about him?

Don Juan: Leave him there: before the dawn comes, early,
          I'll carry him out beneath my cloak
          And leave him at the crossroads.

Laura: Just
          Be careful no one sees you.
          How lucky you were that you didn't come
          A minute earlier! Your friends
240   Were dining here with me. They just
          Had left the house. What if you'd met them!

Don Juan: Laura, did you love him long?

Laura: Who? You must be raving.

Don Juan:	Tell the truth, How many times have you cheated on me While I was gone?
Laura:	What about you, skirt-chaser?
Don Juan:	Tell me. . . . No, we'll talk later.

SCENE III

(*Monument to the knight-commander.*)

Don Juan: All turns out for the best: after killing
Don Carlos unexpectedly, I've hidden here
Dressed as a humble monk — and every day

250   I see my charming widow, and she,
It seems to me, has noticed. Until now
We've held back from each other; but today
I'll say something to her; it's time.
How should I start? "If I may be so bold" . . . or no:
"Señora" . . . bah! Whatever comes to mind,
That's what I'll say, without rehearsing,
An improviser of the song of love . . .
She should already be here. Without her,
I think, the knight-commander must be bored.

260   What a giant he's been made into here!
What shoulders! What a Hercules!
The man himself was small and puny,
If he were here and stood on tiptoe,
His fingertip couldn't reach to his own nose.
When we went out beyond the Escurial,
He stuck himself upon my sword and died
Like a dragonfly upon a pin — but still

He was proud and bold, and stern of spirit . . .
Ah! there she is.

(*Enter Doña Anna.*)

Doña Anna: He's here again. Father,
270   I have disturbed you in your meditations—
              Forgive me.

Don Juan: I should ask forgiveness
              Of you, señora. Perhaps my presence stops you
              From freely pouring out your sorrow.

Doña Anna: No, Father, my sorrow stays within,
              When you are here, my prayers can rise
              To heaven peacefully—I ask
              That you join your voice with them.

Don Juan: I, I to pray with you, Doña Anna!
              Such a portion I have not deserved.
280   I would not dare allow my sinful lips
              To repeat the holy utterance of your prayer—
              I only watch you from afar with reverence,
              And when your head is quietly bowed down,
              Black tresses spilling on the marble's whiteness—
              Then it seems to me an angel comes
              To honor this grave with a secret visit,
              And in my troubled heart I cannot find
              The words to pray. I marvel then in silence
              And think—happy man, whose cold marble
290   Is warmed by her celestial breathing
              And sprinkled with her tears of love.

Doña Anna: What words—how strange!

Don Juan: Señora?

Doña Anna: I . . . you forget yourself.

Don Juan: What? That I
Am an unworthy monk? That, sinner that I am,
My voice should not resound so loudly here?

Doña Anna: I thought . . . I didn't understand . . .

Don Juan: I see: you know it all, you know already!

Doña Anna: What do I know?

Don Juan: It's true, I'm not a monk —
I beg forgiveness, kneeling at your feet.

300 Doña Anna: Oh God! Get up, get up. . . . Who are you?

Don Juan: An unlucky man, victim of a hopeless passion.

Doña Anna: Oh, my God! And here, right by the grave!
Leave now!

Don Juan: Just a minute, Doña Anna,
A single minute!

Doña Anna: If someone came in! . . .

Don Juan: The gate is locked. A single minute!

Doña Anna: Well? What? What do you want?

Don Juan: To die.
Oh, let me die this minute, at your feet,
Let my poor dust be buried in this place,
Not by the dust which is so dear to you,
310 Nor anywhere nearby — some distance off,
There — by the gates — at the very entrance,
So when you come, my gravestone might be brushed
By your light foot or by your dress's hem

When you make your way to that proud grave
To lay your ringlets on it and to weep.

Doña Anna: You've gone mad.

Don Juan: To desire one's end—
Really, Doña Anna, does that show madness?
If I were a madman, I would wish
To stay among the living, for I'd hope
My tender love could touch your heart;
If I were a madman, I would spend
My nights in song beneath your balcony,
Rousing you from sleep with serenades,
I would not have hidden myself, but rather
Would try to have you see me everywhere;
If I were a madman, I would not
Have suffered in silence . . .

Doña Anna: This is what
You call silence?

Don Juan: Chance, Doña Anna,
Chance carried me away. Otherwise
You'd never have known my grievous secret.

Doña Anna: And have you loved me a long time?

Don Juan: A long time or no—I cannot say myself,
I know but this, that only since that time
Have I understood a single instant's value
And known what the word happiness means.

Doña Anna: Leave me—you're a dangerous man.

Don Juan: Dangerous! How?

Doña Anna: I'm frightened hearing you.

Don Juan: I shall be silent then; but do not drive away
             One whose only joy is seeing you.
340   I cherish no presumptuous hopes,
             I ask no sign of favor from you, but still
             I must see you, so long as I am doomed
             To live.

Doña Anna: Leave — this is not the place
             For such words and such madness. Tomorrow
             Come to my house. If you will swear
             To show the same respect to me as now,
             I'll receive you; but after night falls, late —
             I haven't seen anyone since the day
             That I was widowed . . .

Don Juan: Angel Doña Anna!
350   May God comfort you as much as you today
             Have comforted one suffering and unhappy.

Doña Anna: Now leave me.

Don Juan: One minute longer.

Doña Anna: No, then clearly I must go. . . . Besides, my prayers
             Have completely slipped my mind. You distracted me
             With worldly speeches, to which my ears
             Have long been unaccustomed. — Tomorrow
             I will receive you.

Don Juan: I still don't dare believe it,
             I don't dare give myself up to this happiness . . .
             Tomorrow I'll be seeing you! — and not here
360   And not in secret!

Doña Anna: Yes, tomorrow, tomorrow.
              What's your name?

Don Juan: Diego de Calvado.

Doña Anna: Farewell then, Don Diego.

              (*She exits.*)

Don Juan: Leporello!

              (*Leporello enters.*)

Leporello: What can I do for you?

Don Juan: Dear Leporello!
              I'm happy! . . . "Tomorrow, at night, late . . ."
              My Leporello, tomorrow's it — get ready . . .
              I'm happy as a child!

Leporello: You spoke
              With Doña Anna? And perhaps she
              Said a kindly word or two to you,
              Or you gave her your blessing.

370   Don Juan: No, Leporello, no! A rendezvous,
              She named the time and place.

Leporello: Not really!
              Oh widows, you're all the same.

Don Juan: I'm happy!
              I could sing, I'm ready to embrace the whole world.

Leporello: And the knight-commander? What'll he have to say?

Don Juan: What do you think — he's going to be jealous?
              Not likely; he's a reasonable man
              And probably has cooled off some after dying.

Leporello: No; look at his statue.

Don Juan: What about it?

Leporello: It seems as if it's looking at you
380   Angrily.

Don Juan: Leporello, go up to it,
Request it to be so kind as to pay a visit
To me — or no — to Doña Anna, tomorrow.

Leporello: Invite the statue to visit! Why?

Don Juan: Probably not
So we can have a pleasant conversation —
Ask the statue to come to Doña Anna's
Tomorrow late at night to stand
And watch the door.

Leporello: You want to joke,
Think who you're joking with!

Don Juan: Do it.

Leporello: But . . .

Don Juan: Now.

Leporello: Most glorious and handsome statue!
390   My lord Don Juan respectfully requests
The pleasure of your company. . . . My God, I can't,
I'm too afraid.

Don Juan: Coward! I'll show you!

Leporello: All right.
My lord Don Juan requests you to come
Tomorrow late at night to your wife's house
To watch the door . . .

(*The statue nods its head to show agreement.*)

Aiee!

Don Juan: What is it?

Leporello: Aiee, aiee! . . .
Aiee, aiee . . . I'm going to die!

Don Juan: What's happened to you?

Leporello: (Nodding his head)
The statue . . . aiee! . . .

Don Juan: You're nodding your head!

Leporello: No,
Not me, it!

Don Juan: What nonsense are you talking!

Leporello: Go yourself.

Don Juan: So watch me, good-for-nothing.
400   I request, knight-commander, that you pay
A visit to your widow, where I'll be tomorrow,
And stand guard at the door. Well? Are you coming?

(*The statue nods again.*)

Oh God!

Leporello: See? I told you that . . .

Don Juan: Let's go.

SCENE IV

(Doña Anna's chamber. Don Juan and Doña Anna.)

Doña Anna: I have received you, Don Diego; but
I fear it will be wearisome to you
To hear my sorrowful words: a poor widow,
I always am remembering my loss. My tears
And smiles are mingled, like the month of April.
Why are you silent?

Don Juan: I'm speechless with joy,

410   Thinking to myself that I am alone
With the lovely Doña Anna. Here—not there,
Not by the grave of that happy departed one—
And I see you now no longer on your knees
Before your marble spouse.

Doña Anna: Don Diego,
So you're jealous. My husband torments you
Even in his grave?

Don Juan: I shouldn't be jealous.
It was you who chose him.

Doña Anna: No, my mother
Ordered me to marry Don Alvaro.
We were poor, and Don Alvaro rich.

420 Don Juan: Happy man! He laid his empty treasures
At the feet of a goddess, and for that
He tasted heavenly bliss! Oh, if only
I'd known you then, how rapturously
My rank, my wealth, everything I had,
I'd have given for one favorable glance.
I would have been a slave to your sacred will,

Your every whim I would have closely studied,
To fulfill it in advance; so that your life
Would have been enchantment never-ending.

430   Alas!—Fate decreed otherwise for me.

Doña Anna: Diego, stop it; when I listen to you,
I commit a sin—I mustn't love you,
A widow should be faithful to the grave.
If only you knew how much Don Alvaro
Loved me! Oh, surely Don Alvaro
Wouldn't have received an enamoured lady
If he'd been widowed.—He'd have been faithful
To spousal love.

Don Juan: Do not torment my heart,
Doña Anna, by this eternal mentioning

440   Of your husband. You've punished me enough,
Though perhaps the punishment's deserved.

Doña Anna: For what?
There are no holy bonds uniting you
To any other—isn't that so? When you love me,
You do no wrong to me or in Heaven's eyes.

Don Juan: To you! God!

Doña Anna: Can you indeed be guilty
Toward me? Tell me, of what.

Don Juan: No!
No, never.

Doña Anna: Diego, what does this mean?
You've done me a wrong? How, tell me.

Don Juan: No! Not for anything!

Doña Anna: Diego, this is strange:
450   I'm asking you, I order.

Don Juan: No, no.

Doña Anna: Ah! So this is your obedience to my will!
           What was it you said to me just now?
           That you would gladly be my slave.
           I'm getting angry, Diego: answer me,
           What is the wrong you've done me?

Don Juan: I don't dare—
           If I tell, you'll begin to hate me.

Doña Anna: No, no. I forgive you in advance,
           But I wish to know . . .

Don Juan: Don't seek to know
           My terrible and bloody secret.

460 Doña Anna: A terrible secret! You're tormenting me.
           I can't bear not to know—what is it?
           And how could you have injured me?
           I didn't know you—I have no enemies
           And never had any. My husband's killer
           Is the only one.

Don Juan: (*To himself.*)
                            Now it's make or break.
           Tell me, would you know Don Juan,
           That wretched man?

Doña Anna: No, in all my life
           I've never seen him.

Don Juan: In your heart
           Do you nurse hate for him?

Doña Anna: As honor demands.

470   But you're trying to distract me
            From my question, Don Diego —
            I order . . .

Don Juan: What if you should chance
            To meet Don Juan?

Doña Anna: I'd plunge my dagger
            Into the villain's heart.

Don Juan: Doña Anna,
            Where's your dagger? Here's my breast.

Doña Anna: Diego!
            What are you saying?

Don Juan: I am not Diego, I am Juan.

Doña Anna: Oh God! No, it can't be true, I don't believe it.

Don Juan: I'm Don Juan.

Doña Anna: It's a lie.

Don Juan: I killed
            Your husband; and I don't regret it —
480   And there's no repentance in me.

Doña Anna: What am I hearing? No, it can't be, no.

Don Juan: I'm Don Juan, and I'm in love with you.

Doña Anna: (*Falling.*)
            Where am I? . . . Where am I? I feel faint.

Don Juan: Oh God!
            What's happened to her? What's happened, Doña Anna?

Wake up, wake up, open your eyes, look: your Diego,
Your slave is at your feet.

Doña Anna: Leave me alone!

(*Weakly.*)

Oh, you're my enemy — you took away from me
Everything I ever . . .

Don Juan: Lovely being!
I'm ready to give everything in atonement,
490   At your feet I wait to hear your order,
Command — I'll die; command — and then I'll breathe
For only you . . .

Doña Anna: So this is Don Juan . . .

Don Juan: No doubt he's been described to you
As a criminal, a monster. Doña Anna,
The stories, it may be, are partly true,
My weary conscience, may be, bears the burden
Of a heavy load of evil. Indeed, I have
Long followed willingly the path of vice,
But since the moment when I first saw you,
500   It seems to me that I have been reborn.
In loving you, I've come to love the good,
And humbly, for the first time in my life,
I bend my trembling knees before it.

Doña Anna: Oh, Don Juan is eloquent — I know,
I've heard that; he's a cunning tempter.
They say you're a godless profligate,
A very devil. How many poor women
Have you ruined?

Don Juan: Not a single one of them
                          Did I love till now.

Doña Anna: And I should believe
510   That Don Juan really loves for the first time,
                          That he doesn't want to add me to his victims!

Don Juan: Suppose that I had meant to deceive you,
                          Would I admit, would I have said that name
                          Which you can't bear even to hear mentioned?
                          What kind of plot or cunning does that show?

Doña Anna: Who knows you? — But how could you come here?
                          You could be recognized in this house,
                          And then there'd be no escaping death.

Don Juan: What's death? For one sweet instant together
520   Willingly I'd give up my life.

Doña Anna: But how
                          Can you leave this house, reckless man?

Don Juan: And you concern yourself about the life
                          Of poor Juan! So there is no hate
                          Within your heavenly soul, Doña Anna?

Doña Anna: Ah, if only I could hate you!
                          But all the same we have to part.

Don Juan: When will we meet again?

Doña Anna: I don't know.
                          Sometime.

Don Juan: Tomorrow?

Doña Anna: Then where?

Don Juan: Here.

Doña Anna: Oh Don Juan, how weak of heart I am.

530 Don Juan: Seal your pardon with a peaceful kiss.

Doña Anna: It's time now, go.

Don Juan: A single kiss, cold, peaceful . . .

Doña Anna: How importunate you are! Well, there it is.
What's that noise outside? . . . Oh, hide, Don Juan.

Don Juan: Farewell till our next meeting, my beloved.

(*He goes out and runs back in.*)

Ah! . . .

Doña Anna: What's happened? Ah! . . .

*(The statue of the knight-commander enters.
Doña Anna falls.)*

Statue: You bade me, I have
come.

Don Juan: God in Heaven! Doña Anna!

Statue: Leave her,
All is finished. You quake, Don Juan.

Don Juan: I? — no. I bid you come, I'm glad to see you.

Statue: Give me your hand.

Don Juan: Here . . . oh, it's heavy,
540   The stony grip of his right hand!
Leave me alone, let go — let go of me . . .
I am undone — it's finished — Doña Anna!

(They descend.)

A Feast During the Plague

(From Wilson's tragedy *The City of the Plague*)

(*A street. A table, set. A number of men and women feasting.*)

Young Man: Mr. Chairman! I call to mind
Someone whom we all know well,
A man whose jokes and funny stories,
Witty retorts and observations,
So biting in their mock pomposity,
Have enlivened our table talk
And driven away the gloom that now
The plague, our guest, is shedding
Over the most brilliant minds.
10　　　　Two days ago our laughter crowned

His stories; it isn't possible
That in our merry feasting we should
Forget Jackson. Here's his chair,
Sitting empty, as if waiting for
A good companion — but he's gone away
To a cold lodging underground . . .
Although that tongue of wondrous eloquence
Has not yet fallen silent in the grave;
But many of us still live, and we
20   Have no cause to be grieving. So
I propose we drink a toast to him
With glasses clinking and with shouts
As if he were alive.

Chairman: He was the first
Of our group to go. In silence
We'll drink to honor him.

Young Man: So be it!

(*All drink silently.*)

Chairman: Your voice, my dear, brings forth the songs
Of your native land with rude perfection;
Sing, Mary, something sad and haunting,
To make us turn again to our merrymaking
30   With a wilder spirit, like one who is seized
And carried away by some unearthly vision.

Mary: (Sings.)
Not so long ago our village
Had fair fame the country round.
The church was full of folk on Sunday
When the steeple bell would sound.
In the schoolroom children's voices

Read their lessons true and clear.
In the field the sickles glittered,
And the scythe mowed down the ear.

40   Now the church is mute and empty,
Weeds within the schoolyard grow,
No reaper cuts the whitened grain,
To the woods no huntsmen go.
Like a burned, abandoned homestead
Silently our village stands.
The only bustle's in the graveyard—
It has work for every hand!

For the dead are carried out
To burials that never cease,
50   The living pray in fear and trembling,
"To their souls, O Lord, give peace."
There's hardly room for all the graves:
Once each one its space could keep,
Now they're huddled all together
Like a flock of frightened sheep.

If my springtime too is blighted,
If the grave my lot must be,
You whom I have loved so long,
Whose love was always joy to me—
60   Oh, come not near then to your Jenny,
No last kiss on her pale lips lay,
Watch, but watch you from afar off
When they bear her corpse away!

Then leave behind our stricken village!
Find yourself some place apart
Where these torments may be lightened,
And there ease your weary heart.

When the plague ends — then come visit
Where my poor dust found its rest,
70   And Jenny will be true to Edmund
E'en in her place among the blest!

Chairman: Thank you, melancholy Mary,
Thank you for that plaintive song!
In earlier days the plague, it's clear,
Visited your native hills and dales
And moans of sorrow then were heard
Along those brooks and streams which now
Flow so peaceful and so merry
Through your land's rude paradise.
80   That gloomy year, in which there fell so many
Among the brave, the beautiful and good,
Has hardly left a trace, except the memory
Of simple shepherds, singing an old song,
A sad and sweet one. . . . Nothing else
Can move us so amid our merrymaking
As such a lingering, heart-repeated sound!

Mary: Oh, if only I had never sung
To anyone outside my parents' croft!
How they loved to listen to their Mary;
90   It seems to me that I can hear myself
Singing in the house where I was born.
My voice was sweeter then — it was
The voice of innocence . . .

Louisa: Now those songs
Are hopelessly passé. But there are still
Some fools who like to melt when women cry,
Who'll swallow it hook, line, and sinker.
She's decided that her tearful look

Can't be resisted — if that's what she thought
About her laugh, no doubt we'd see her
Grinning all the time. Walsingham liked
The weepy northern beauties — so of course
She's got to moan and groan. I can't stand
The jaundice-yellow hair of these Scotch girls.

Chairman: Listen. I hear the creak of wheels!

(*A wagon filled with bodies passes. A black man is driving.*)

Ah! Louisa's fainted; judging from her words,
I'd thought she had a mannish heart.
But so it is: the cruel are weaker than the tender,
And fear still lives in souls worn out by passions.
Mary, dash water in her face. She's coming to.

Mary: Sister of my shame and sorrow,
Lean upon my breast.

Louisa: (*Reviving*)

            I dreamed I saw
A hideous demon, black all over, with white eyes . . .
He called me to his wagon. Lying in it
Were the dead — and they were muttering
In some hideous, unknown language.
Tell me: was it after all a dream?
Did the wagon pass?

Young Man: Well, Louisa,
Cheer up — although the street's all ours,
An untrafficked hiding-place from death
Where our revels are disturbed by no one,
Still, you must know: that black wagon
Has the right to go to any place.
We have to let it through! But listen:

Walsingham, to cut off all these quarrels
And clear away these female fainting fits,
Sing us a song—a bold and lively song,
No lamentation of the Scottish Muse—
A rowdy song, a song in Bacchus's mode,
One inspired by foaming goblets!

130 Chairman: I don't know one like that—here's what I'll sing:
A hymn in honor of the Plague. I wrote it
Late last night, after we had parted.
I found I had a strange poetic impulse
For the first time in my life! So listen:
My harsh voice will befit the song.

Many Voices: A hymn in honor of the Plague! Let's hear it!
A hymn in honor of the Plague! Splendid! Bravo!

Chairman: (Sings.)
When Winter in his boisterous might
Leads his legions forth to fight,
140 Attacking us with ice and snow,
We're ready for him—we gather near
Beside the crackling fire's warm glow,
And there we feast and keep good cheer.

Now Pestilence, that queen of dread,
In triumph rides among the dead.
And as her victims' ranks increase
Each day, each night her burial spade
Knocks at our windows without cease . . .
What can we do? Where look for aid?

150 Old Man Winter we've beat back;
That's how we'll meet the Plague's attack!
We'll light the fire and fill the cup

And pass it round—a merry scene!
And after we have all drunk up,
We'll sing: All hail to thee, dread queen!

There's rapture in the bullets' flight
And on the mountain's treacherous height,
And on a ship's deck far from land
When skies grow dark and waves swell high,
And in Sahara's blowing sand,
And when the pestilence is nigh.

All, all that threatens to destroy
Fills mortal hearts with secret joy
Beyond our power to explain—

Perhaps it bodes eternal life!
And blest is he who can attain
That ecstasy in storm and strife!

So — for the Plague a hearty cheer!
The grave's dark doesn't make us fear,
170   If Death calls us — we'll answer coldly.
We'll join in quaffing from the keg,
Rose-maidens' scents we drink in boldly,
Scents, it may be — full of the Plague!

Priest: A godless feast, befitting godless madmen!
Your feasting and your shameless songs
Mock at and profane the gloomy peace
Spread everywhere by death and desolation!
Amidst the horror of the mournful burials,
Amidst pale faces I pray at the graveyard,
180   And your hateful shouts and cries of revelry
Disturb the silence of the tomb — because of you,
The earth itself trembles over the dead bodies!
If the prayers of so many reverend men and women
Had not consecrated the common gravepit,
I would have thought that devils even now
Were torturing some ruined, godless soul,
Laughing as they dragged it to outer darkness.

Several Voices: He talks about Hell like a real expert!
Get going, old man! Hit the road!

190   Priest: I adjure you by the holy blood
Of the Savior crucified for us:
Halt this monstrous feast, if ever
You hope to meet again in Heaven
The souls of those whom you have lost.
Go, each of you, to your homes!

Chairman: Our homes
                    Are sorrowful—youth loves gaiety.

Priest: Is that you, Walsingham? Are you the same man
                    Who just three weeks ago dropped to your knees,
                    Embracing your mother's body as you wept,
200   And howling beat your fists upon her grave?
                    Or do you think she isn't crying now,
                    Shedding bitter tears in Heaven itself,
                    To see her son caught up in reveling
                    At a shameless feast, to hear your voice
                    Singing like one possessed, amidst
                    Holy prayers and deep-felt sighs?
                    Follow me!

Chairman: Why have you come here
                    To trouble me? I cannot, I must not
                    Follow after you: I am bound here
210   By despair, by terrible remembrance,
                    By the knowledge of my lawlessness,
                    And by horror of that dead emptiness
                    Which greets me now in my own house—
                    And by the novelty of these furious revels,
                    And by the blessed poison of this cup,
                    And by the caresses—God forgive me—
                    Of a being, ruined, but still dear . . .
                    My mother's shade will not call me away
                    From here—it's too late—I hear your voice
220   Calling me—I recognize your striving
                    To save me. . . . Old man, go in peace;
                    But accursed may he be who follows you!

Many Voices: Bravo, bravo! Mr. Chairman!
                    There's a sermon for you! Take a hike!

Priest: Matilda's pure soul calls you!

Chairman: (Stands.)
              Swear to me, lifting your pale
              And withered hand to Heaven, to leave
              That name forever silenced in the grave!
              Oh, if only I could hide this sight
230   From her immortal eyes! Once
              She thought me pure, proud, free—
              And found paradise in my embrace . . .
              Where am I? Holy child of light! I see
              You there, where my fallen spirit
              Will never reach . . .

Woman's Voice: He's gone mad—
              He's raving about his buried wife!

Priest: Let's go, let's go . . .

Chairman: Father, for God's sake
              Leave me!

Priest: God save you!
              Farewell, my son.

              (*He exits. The feast continues. The Chairman remains,
              plunged in deep contemplation.*)

Critical Essays

The Seduction of Power: *The Miserly Knight*

THE THEME OF inner conflict that dominates all the "little tragedies" is evident in the very title of the first of them, *The Miserly Knight*. Traditionally, the miser thinks of nothing but holding on to and increasing his hoard of money. Nothing distracts him from his own self-interest, which he understands in the narrowest possible terms. By contrast, in theory if not in practice, a knight was a supremely disinterested figure, someone who applied his strength, not to advancing himself, but to defending worthy causes or protecting the weak. In his eyes, selfishness or cowardice or lack of integrity was not merely a sin; it was a stain upon his knightly honor. Yet in practice, the substance of honor was all too readily replaced by the mere show of it: the honor of being admired and deferred to by others, an honor conferred by rank, wealth, and power. And from this debased concept of honor as resting upon wealth and power, it was only a short step to the naked pursuit of wealth and power for their own sake, with no regard for justice.

Bearing this in mind, one can see that *The Miserly Knight* has the most schematic characterization of all the "little tragedies." Aside from the minor figure of Albert's servant, each of the secondary characters represents one of these attitudes toward knightly honor. The Duke, the feudal lord, is associated with the chivalrous ideal, with self-restraint and the service of justice; Albert is associated with the concept of purely external honor, honor that depends on what others think of him, and is all too aware of how much that depends on money; and the Jewish moneylender Solomon lays no claim to honor at all, but is frankly and solely interested in money, whatever he may have to do to obtain it. The play's central character, the Baron, has within him aspects of all three of these secondary roles: he is unscrupulous in amassing gold but is genuinely tormented by his awareness of his unjust acts; he desires to be regarded as a loyal knight and an honorable man while acting in a way that his lord and his society cannot condone. His gold has given him the vision of a power that is the opposite of knightly—a power without restraint, without justice—and his ambivalence toward this vision, which at once attracts and appalls him, will ultimately prove catastrophic to him.

A reader encountering *The Miserly Knight* for the first time might pardonably think during its first scene that the title referred to Albert. His obsession with money becomes clear in the very first lines, in which he voices his fury at the tournament opponent who damaged his helmet, and thus required him to go to the expense of replacing it. His valet suggests that he has fairly repaid this offense by gravely wounding his opponent, but for Albert physical injury means nothing compared to money:

> Still, he lost nothing by it;
> His breastplate of Venetian steel is whole,

And his chest's his own; it costs him nothing;
He won't be buying himself another.

This is not mere callousness toward an enemy, for Albert speaks of his own physical safety with the same contempt—rather than have an opponent damage his helmet, it would be "better if he had pierced my head."

But, as Albert's monologue quickly makes clear, it is not money itself that he craves. Rather, he sees money as a necessary means to the end which he truly desires: the recognition and admiration of the court for his distinction as a knight. Thus, when Albert defeats Count Delorge in the tournament, the law of arms gives Albert the right either to claim the defeated man's horse and armor, or to name a price for their ransom. Albert gives up this right—not, however, out of magnanimity, as would be truly chivalrous, but simply out of a desire to appear magnanimous "in front of ladies and the Duke." When Albert comes to the ducal court without the luxurious clothes that his fellow noblemen are wearing, the code of chivalry would tell him that gentle birth and conduct are the true measure of worth, that a wealthy churl is still a churl, and a poor knight still a knight. Instead, Albert is galled by what he sees as his disreputably poor appearance, and tries to make up for it with the unchivalrous tactic of a lie, and worse yet, a lie to his honored lord. One suspects that his generosity to the sick blacksmith, to whom he sends his last bottle of wine, is of a piece with his generosity to his defeated opponent—a way of getting talked about. It is significant that in Pushkin's manuscript the original word meaning "miller" is replaced by one meaning "smith"[1]—a skillful armorer, unlike a miller, would come into contact with many noblemen, and his words of praise would be likely to reach the desired audience.

Albert is caught in a paradox: to make the spectacular, attention-getting gestures that will win him the reputation and esteem he craves, he needs money; but with his limited financial resources, making such gestures even occasionally forces him to be preoccupied with their cost—and concern over money is something that the society he wishes to impress regards as ignoble. He is painfully aware of this paradox:

When Delorge with his heavy lance
Pierced my helm and galloped on past,
And I bareheaded turned and spurred
My Emir, flew like a whirlwind
And flung the count some twenty paces
Like a page boy; when all the ladies
Rose from their seats, when Clotild herself,
Who'd covered her eyes, couldn't help but shout,
And the heralds paid honors to my blow—
No one then thought about the reason
For my valor and my wondrous strength!
I was seized by fury at my damaged helmet,
What's to blame for my heroism?—miserliness.

Albert thus sees himself as a man who has been unfairly put in a false position, deprived of the honor to which he is rightfully entitled. As a knight, he needs a new helmet and a sound horse; having made the public gesture of renouncing his defeated opponent's arms and horse, he must obtain the necessary money in some other manner. The only method he can come up with is one that even further deepens his sense of frustration and unjust injury: the ignominious expedient of dealing with a Jewish moneylender. Albert is so blinded by his fury, so convinced that it is simply his right to have the money he desires, that it never crosses his mind that a moneylender is in the business in order to make money, and is not likely to welcome a would-be borrower whose ability to repay is doubtful. If promises—redeemable at some vague and indefinite future—aren't good enough for Solomon, threats will have to be used instead. Indeed, given Albert's state of violent exasperation, even when he does manage to remember for a moment that it

would be prudent to be polite to Solomon, his attempted smile at once
becomes a vicious sneer:

Albert:　　　Who's there?

Jew:　　　　　　　　Your humble servant.

Albert:　　　　　　　　　　　　Ah, friend!
　　　　　You damned Jew, honorable Solomon,
　　　　　Come over here; so — you, I hear,
　　　　　Don't believe in credit.

Jew:　　　　　　　　　　Ah, merciful knight,
　　　　　I swear to you: I'd be glad . . . truly, I can't.
　　　　　Where would I get money? I've ruined myself
　　　　　Through my zeal for always helping knights.
　　　　　No one repays. I wanted to ask you
　　　　　If you couldn't give me even just part . . .

Albert:　　　　　　　　　　　　Robber!
　　　　　If I had any money, would I be
　　　　　Fooling around with you? Enough,
　　　　　Don't be stubborn, my dear Solomon;
　　　　　Give me some gold. Send me a hundred pieces
　　　　　Before I have you searched.

While Albert is preoccupied by esteem and status, clearly no con-
sideration could be further from his interlocutor's mind. As a practi-
tioner of a despised religion (Judaism) and as a member of a despised
profession (moneylending), Solomon has already forfeited any claim
to respect from someone of Albert's social position. And he has no
concern about debasing himself further (as Albert would see it) by responding to Albert's threats, not with self-assertion, but with a whin-
ing, all-too-obviously mendacious tone.

Nevertheless, Albert's contempt for Solomon is not altogether jus-
tified. It would not cross Albert's mind, but Solomon clearly has cour-

age, even if not a knightly kind. In dealing with lords such as Albert—
and Solomon's speech indicates that he has such dealings regularly
—the possibility that they might not repay him is the least of his dangers. Albert's threats to seize him and have him searched, or even to
have him hanged at the castle gates, are not mere empty words; both
of them know that no feudal lord would waste much effort on punish-
ing a nobleman accused of nothing more serious than using violence
against a Jew. And, in contrast to Albert's impetuousness, Solomon
has the potentially valuable qualities—unfortunately put to ill use—
of foresight and patience in conceiving and carrying out a plan. Since
we have already learned even before he appears on stage that Solomon
has refused to loan Albert any more money, the question arises: why
does he then come in person to Albert? The only logical explanation
is that he has come solely in order to propose to Albert that the latter
poison his father—a type of proposal that one cannot send through
servants or intermediaries. Ignoring Albert's abuse, Solomon steadily
steers their conversation in the appropriate direction: he links his refusal to lend to Albert over concern about when, or even if, Albert will
inherit his father's money; he listens willingly to Albert's expression
of scorn and contempt for his father, expresses the wish that Albert
inherit soon, and gets Albert's open approval of this wish. Only then,
with the ground well-prepared, does he say, as if offhandedly: "It occurred to me there is / A certain means . . ." Having thus gotten Albert's
attention, Solomon still proceeds cautiously, methodically: he knows
a certain apothecary; this apothecary sells drops; these drops have a
particular effect. With each sentence, he takes one more cautious step
across what may yet prove to be thin ice. Only when Albert completely
fails to grasp what is being suggested to him does Solomon finally state
his purpose, in a still-veiled but nevertheless unmistakable form:

Albert: And so? Instead of loaning money,
              You're offering me two hundred vials of poison,
              At one gold piece per vial. Is that it?

Jew: You're pleased to have your joke at my expense—
         No; I meant . . . perhaps you . . . well, I thought
         The Baron's time had come to die.

Solomon is apparently oblivious to the irony in the contrast between his earlier pious observation that a man's days are numbered by Another and his current proposal that he, or rather Albert, take steps to number the Baron's days. The moneylender's attitude is reminiscent of the traditional image of the mafioso: piety and respectability are both good things, but business is business; if you have to kill somebody to make money, you kill him; there's no point in being sentimental about it.

   Such an attitude leaves Solomon unprepared to deal with a man like Albert, for whom the primary concern is not money, but his bizarre sense of honor—an honor based not upon his own inner sentiments, but upon a constant awareness of what type of conduct is approved or disapproved of by society. Albert feels no guilt about hating his father or wishing for his father's death; but he knows that in society's eyes parricide is one of the most horrible crimes possible, and that the man who commits it has lost any claim to respect. Indeed, Albert feels dishonored simply by the fact that a despised Jew made such a proposal to him, just as a noblewoman's reputation would be damaged by the inappropriate familiarity of a peasant even if she repudiated his advances. This threat to Albert's self-image and self-esteem causes him to lose what little self-control he has: he threatens to have Solomon hanged and drives him out, ignoring Solomon's placatory offer of money—the very offer which Albert would gladly have taken a few minutes earlier. Even when Albert recovers enough self-possession to remember that he is still facing the same monetary problems that originally made him turn to Solomon, even when he experiences a moment of regret for not having taken the money which was offered, he nevertheless feels that it has now become impossible for him to take anything from Solomon—his money has become blood money, tainted, dishonoring anyone who accepts it:

> To have a Jew dare
> Propose that to me! Bring me a glass of wine,
> I'm shaking like a leaf. . .But I still need money.
> John, go catch up with that damned Jew
> And take his gold. And bring the inkwell here.
> I'll give him a receipt, the crook—but don't
> Bring that Judas in here. . . . No, wait.
> His gold pieces will stink of poison,
> Like his kinsman's silver did . . .

Now deprived even of the assistance of a moneylender, Albert takes a desperate decision: to swallow the humiliation of revealing his poverty to his feudal lord the Duke, in return for the Duke's order to his father to support him in a manner fitting to his social position.

This entire first scene is a model of dramatic economy: in less than 160 lines, Pushkin has delineated two memorable characters, Albert and Solomon; laid the groundwork for the decisive confrontation of the third scene; and established the as-yet-unseen Baron as a presence in our minds. His extraordinary miserliness has already evoked comments from both Solomon and Albert, each of whom explains it in a characteristic manner. The unimaginative Solomon—expressing himself in a proverbial style worthy of his Biblical namesake—sees it as merely a financial expression of the prudence natural to the old, as rashness is to the young:

> . . . Money
> Is always, whatever our age, useful to us;
> But a young man sees it as a servant
> And doesn't hesitate to send it far and wide.
> An old man sees it as a trusty friend
> And guards it as the apple of his eye.

By contrast, Albert, with his pride in his knightly rank and his consciousness of its prerogatives, sees his father's miserliness as the result of the same contemptible meanness of spirit, the same innate servility, which to a medieval lord would be the natural trait of peasants or worse:

> Oh, for my father money's not a servant
> Or a friend, but a master; he himself serves it.
> And serves it — how? like an Algerian slave,
> Like a dog on a chain. A kennel with no heat
> Is his home, he drinks water, eats dry crusts,
> He never sleeps at night, just runs and barks.
> And the gold lies there resting peacefully
> In the chests . . .

Our first sight of the Baron, however, quickly establishes how seriously limited both Solomon's and Albert's explanations of his motives are. In contrast to Solomon's assessment, the Baron's first words reveal not an old man's excess of caution, but an uncontrolled passion for money which he himself compares to a sexual craving:

> Like a young skirt-chaser who waits for when
> He'll meet his bimbo — some tramp on the make,
> Or some fool he's snowed — that's how all day
> I wait for the minute I go down
> Into my secret vault, to the faithful chests.

But in contrast to the uncontrolled emotions of his son, the Baron's passion is focused methodically and unwaveringly on his single goal, day after day and year after year. The actions which, taken individually, Albert sees as mean and petty, are seen by the Baron as small parts of an overall strategy — a strategy which, so far from being servile, could be conceived and carried through only by a man of extraordinary willpower and ambition:

> Today's a happy day! Now I can open
> The sixth chest (the one that's not full yet)
> And pour in a handful of piled-up gold.
> Not much, it seems, but little by little
> The treasure grows. Once I read
> About a king who ordered his men
> To bring, each one, a handful of earth,
> And a mighty hill rose up — and the king
> Could gaze down merrily from that height
> Upon the valleys, covered with white tents,
> And on the sea, where ships were sailing.
> Thus I, bringing my poor handfuls one by one,
> Bearing my accustomed tribute to my vault,
> Have built up my hill — and from its height
> I can gaze on all that's in my power.
> What's not in my power? From here,
> Like a demon I can rule the world.

Power without limits, power without justice: this is the idea that has seized the Baron's imagination. Albert's callous self-preoccupation, so strikingly shown in the first scene, appears positively childish and trifling compared to the Baron's demand for power. Albert's ambition is simply to gain the respect of those around him by his pre-eminence as a knight, a role that is encouraged by the structure of his society and would be entirely within his reach were it not for his financial difficulties. By contrast, the Baron's ambition is to achieve a pre-eminence so vast and multifaceted that Albert could not even dream of it. While Albert would be satisfied merely to be able to appear at the Duke's feast in silk and satin like the other courtiers, the Baron starts by imagining himself in luxury worthy of a Louis XIV:

If I just want it—palaces will spring up;
Into my splendid gardens there will dance
A company of playful nymphs . . .

But the conventional trappings of mere wealth—even the wealth of a monarch—are not enough for the Baron. He wants power; and power is measured by the greatness of what it has subdued. Thus his thoughts turn to art, which has long claimed the right to pass its own sentence of praise or blame upon the great men of its time. This power, which has maintained its independence and its greatness for so many centuries, now must also yield to the Baron:

The Muses too will bring me tribute,
Free genius will become my slave . . .

And even this is not enough to satisfy his hunger for power. Like a proto-Nietzschean superman, the Baron imagines himself "beyond good and evil." The rules of morality will have no claim on him; rather virtue and vice will be equally subject to him, and he will choose between them as he pleases. Indeed, so complete will his control over evil be, so doglike its devotion to him, that he will never have to actually perform an evil deed, or even to give a command that it be performed; rather, his unspoken wish will be anticipated:

. . . virtue and unsleeping toil
Will meekly look to me for their reward.
Just let me whistle—bloodstained villainy
Obediently and timidly will crawl to me
And lick my hand, and peer into my eyes,
Looking for a sign of my will there . . .

While the Baron takes pleasure in telling himself what he could do, he never actually does (or tries to do) any of it. If he did so, of course, he would quickly encounter the constraints of the real world, where palaces take years to build no matter how many laborers one can hire, and where no matter how carefully the official court histories are compiled, a Tacitus is likely to appear. The necessary condition of the Baron's absolute supremacy is that it should exist only in his imagination. But so far from acknowledging this as a limitation, the Baron convinces himself that this is actually a strength — he is above interesting himself in all those grubby affairs that occupy mere ordinary mortals:

> I stand above desire; I am calm;
> I know my might; this knowledge
> Is enough for me . . .

The only real activity which he concerns himself with, the only desire to which he will admit, is the accumulation of more gold — the foundation of his power. It is no wonder that he sees himself as ruling "like a demon"; for like a demon, he has rejected even the slightest claim of love or compassion. Not only does he have no genuine concern for others; unlike his son, he does not even feel the need to make a pretense of such concern. Albert with his vanity would have forgiven a widow's debt, if not out of genuine pity, at least as a display of magnanimity; the Baron only congratulates himself for not being fooled by what he sees as her sham despair. Albert would see himself as dishonored for accepting Solomon's money after hearing Solomon's proposal that he poison his father; the Baron feels no shame over the crime which he assumes Thibault has committed in order to get money to pay his debt. Indeed, the Baron does not try in any way to downplay or rationalize the suffering he has caused, and if anything exaggerates it:

> If all the blood, sweat, and tears once shed
> For all that's stored in here, could now pour forth

From the earth's bowels in one sudden gush,
There'd be a second Flood — and I would suffocate
Inside my faithful vault. But enough.

The Baron's systematically unscrupulous and inhuman pursuit of
wealth is reminiscent of Solomon; but his mental state is far different
from that of the Jewish moneylender. Solomon, as we have seen, is
not so much immoral as amoral; moral considerations simply have no
meaning to him. The Baron, as a knight, knows what justice is, and is
well aware of the immorality of his actions; but the desire for power,
and the avarice to which it has given rise, has become such an irresistible lure for him that he willingly does what he knows is wrong:

Every single time, when I start to open
A chest, I feel feverish and tremble.
Not from fear (no! what should I fear?
I have my sword; my tempered blade
Will answer for the gold), but from some sense,
Mysterious and dread, which grips my heart . . .
Doctors assure us that there are people
Who find pleasure in committing murder.
When I put the key into the lock, then
I feel what such a one must feel, plunging
His knife into a victim; pleasure
And horror mixed in one.

Given the Baron's earlier comparison of himself to a man in an illicit
sexual liaison, one does not have to be a Freudian to note the sugges-
tiveness of the imagery of a key inserted into a lock or a knife plunged
into a body. And the Baron's insertion of the key evokes a cry of ecstatic
consummation — "My bliss!" — followed by a release of tension:

There, now you've roamed enough throughout the world,
Serving the passions and needs of men,
Sleep now, the sleep of strength and peace . . .

The quasi-sexual dimension of the relationship between the Baron and
his gold is reinforced by the parallel language used in this play to describe the Baron's passion for his gold and in *The Stone Guest* to describe the passion of the knight-commander for Doña Anna. Just as
the Baron carefully locks his gold into his chests and guards the keys, so
Don Juan notes that "Doña Anna always was kept locked up inside, /
None of us have ever so much as seen her." The Baron wishes that

> . . . from my grave
> I could arise, a ghostly watchman,
> And sit upon the chest, and guard my treasures
> Against the living . . .

which is precisely what Don Juan challenges the dead knight-
commander to do: to "stand guard at the door" in order to prevent his
treasured Doña Anna from being stolen from him by a living man. But
while the knight-commander has a rightful claim upon the loyalty of
Doña Anna, the Baron has no rightful claim to gold which he himself
realizes was obtained unjustly: metaphorically speaking, it is not a wife
but either a "tramp" or a "fool," a seductress or a seduced woman.

However, there is a significant difference between a physical passion
and a passion of the imagination such as the Baron's: while a physical passion could be at least temporarily sated by possession for the
Baron, possession of his gold does not satisfy his desire, but inflames
it further. Having experienced the rapture of opening one chest, he
wants an even greater rapture: he opens all six at once. Even then, his
present enjoyment is not enough for him; he must imagine it continuing into the indefinite future. And there is where his imagination runs
up against a rude check. The Baron may boast that "To me all things

submit, and I—to none," but he knows that there is still one force more powerful than he—death. The Baron fears death, not in the way one might have expected a medieval man to do, not as the time when he must pay for his sins. Rather, he has so thoroughly identified his very life with the acquisition and hoarding of his treasure that he fears death as the force that will turn his treasure over to his heir, who will spend it. In the Baron's fevered imagination, the perfectly normal and lawful phenomenon of an heir taking possession of his estate becomes the equivalent of barbarians pillaging a conquered empire:

> After stealing the keys from my dead body,
> He'll laugh as he throws open all the chests.
> And all my treasures will flow out
> And pour through the holes of satin pockets.
> He'll break into bits the sacred vessels,
> Let dirt drink up the coronation oil—
> He'll squander it. . . . And by what right?

Given the means by which the Baron himself acquired his fortune, the logical question would be, "By what right do *you* possess it?" But to the Baron, "right" no longer means law or justice, as it would have when he was a knight at the Duke's court; now it means power. In the Baron's eyes, the one who has the "right" to possess is the one who has the greatest and most unconquerable will to possess. And clearly this is the Baron, who has shown his strength of will not only in his voluntary acceptance of the physical and mental privations—"What cares day after day, what sleepless nights"—at which his son sneers, but through his prolonged endurance of what can only be called self-inflicted spiritual suffering. In the Baron's demonically perverse logic, the torments of conscience he experiences, the very torments that should show that his avarice is wrong, instead become the grounds for asserting that his possession is "right":

> . . . Or will my son say
> That my heart's long overgrown with moss,
> That I feel no desire, that even my conscience
> Never gnawed at me, my conscience,
> That beast with claws that tear my heart — my conscience,
> That guest I didn't invite, a wearying companion,
> That harsh demanding creditor, that witch
> Who makes the moon hide and who troubles graves,
> Making them give up their dead? . . .
> No, first suffer through piling up your own wealth,
> And then let's see if some unhappy man
> Will come and squander what you got by blood.

In this extraordinary passage, we see the full Shakespearean majesty of the Baron's nature. Precisely because he does have a powerful consciousness of justice, and because he deliberately corrupts himself by ignoring that consciousness, he is an immeasurably greater and at the same time far more terrifying figure than a mere common criminal like Solomon: "Lilies that fester smell far worse than weeds." As the Baron gives himself up to his obsession, the power of his spirit grows ever greater, but its focus become ever narrower, until the only form of existence he can imagine or desire even after death is not Heaven, but merely a continuation of the present:

> . . . oh, if from my grave
> I could arise, a ghostly watchman,
> And sit upon the chest, and guard my treasures
> Against the living, as I guard them now!

Just as the first scene closes with Albert's resolution to force his father to give up some money to him, so the second closes with the Baron's resolution to do everything within human power — and indeed more, if he could—not to give up any of his money to his son. Clearly, the two are on a collision course, and as the third scene opens, this collision is imminent:

Albert: Believe me, my lord, I have long borne
            The shame of bitter poverty. Were my need not great,
            You would not have heard my complaint.
Duke: I do believe you: a noble knight
            Such as yourself, would not accuse his father
            Unless his need was great. Few men are so corrupt . . .
            Don't fear; I'll urge your father to act honorably,
            But I'll do it in private, without scandal.
            I expect him soon. It's a long time since I've seen him.
            He and my grandfather were friends. I remember,
            When I was just a boy still, how
            He'd lift me up and set me on his steed
            And put his heavy helmet on me—it covered me
            As if it were a church bell.
            (*Looks out the window.*)
                          Who's that?
     Is it he?

The Duke thus makes his appearance as an ideal knightly figure: someone who is engaged in the disinterested pursuit of justice, someone who is prepared to seek the right and to uphold it. And from his first speech, we recognize the Duke as a different character from the previous major speakers: Albert, Solomon, and the Baron. All three of them are preoccupied with themselves, their own schemes, desires, and ambitions; for all three, other people are expendable. The Duke, by contrast, is genuinely interested in other human beings. He observes their natures and actions, and seeks to understand them. And he is capable of putting himself in another's position, of sparing another's feelings.

One suspects that any of the other three major characters, if they even were capable of consciously recognizing this trait of the Duke's, would merely dismiss it as a weakness; and yet the Duke, who can hardly be more than five or ten years older than Albert, radiates a calm, confident authority. He has no doubt that he can issue a polite but firm command to a baron who was already a powerful man when he himself was yet a child and have that command obeyed. Indeed, he is so confident that he can even afford to laugh at himself—something it is impossible to imagine any of the other characters doing—as he pictures himself as the baron must have seen him, an excited small boy in a ludicrously oversized adult helmet. He is, in short, a type which we recognize from the Duke of Vienna in *Measure for Measure,* from the rightful Duke in *As You Like It,* and even from Henry in *King Henry V:* the ideal Renaissance ruler, at once affable and commanding, genuinely sympathetic toward his subjects, yet always aware of the responsibilities of office that separate him from them. Significantly, the Duke speaks of his insignia of office as not a coronet, but a chain: he may not simply do what he wishes, but must restrain himself. A subject may give in to his passions; a ruler may not.

Despite the impressiveness of such a figure as the Duke, one still wonders whether he is a match for the fierce, ambitious, obsessed man whom we saw in the second scene. And then, to our astonishment, we see—not the Baron we know, but a meek, self-deprecating, pathetically loyal old man:

> I'm an old man now, my lord; what should
> I do at court? You're young, you love
> Tournaments and fêtes. But for such things I
> Am no longer suited. If God sends war, then I
> Am ready to climb wheezing onto my horse;
> I'll still find strength enough to draw
> My old sword for you with a trembling arm.

Of course there is an element of deliberate cunning in the Baron's speech, an attempt to deflect any suggestion that he take part in the luxurious—and expensive—life of the court. Yet the surprise remains: could one have imagined the Baron of the second scene, who boasted of ruling the world like a demon, speaking to anyone in so deferential a manner? But when he is outside the isolated and unreal world of his treasure vault, in the atmosphere of the court he remembers from his youth, so caught up in his memories of his friendship with the former Duke that he refers to his current lord as "that kid" and then hastily corrects his lack of reverence to "you, that is"—at such a moment his personality to some degree reverts to the knight that he was in his youth. In contrast to Albert, who thinks of fighting as something that one does in one's own interest, for the sake of one's glory and reputation, the Baron professes a genuinely knightly willingness to endure hardship and danger with no reward to himself, simply out of loyalty to his lord.

The Baron thus is caught in a dilemma: as a miser, he wants to refuse any command that involves spending money; but as a knight that he cannot conceive of defying his lord directly. So he tries to evade the Duke's urging that he send his son to court by devising one excuse after another as to why his son is unfit for such an honor. And here is where we see the full power of the Duke's patience: the Duke calmly accepts at face value each of the Baron's excuses despite the fact that, since he is acquainted with Albert, he already knows that these excuses are lies; and by taking the Baron's words at face value and discrediting them on their own terms, the Duke politely but inexorably forces the Baron into a corner. The Baron, realizing that no story that he can come up with will be capable of withstanding the Duke's judicious response, tries to take refuge in silence or short, uninformative statements. This tactic, however, does not discourage the iron patience of the Duke, and finally, unable to think of any other way to justify himself before his unyielding questioner, the Baron desperately flings an accusation at his son which he knows to be false:

Duke: I command: tell me the reason
             For your refusal.
Baron: I'm angered at
             My son.
Duke: Why?
Baron: For his wicked crime.
Duke: And what, tell me, was that?
Baron: Spare me, Duke . . .
Duke: This is very strange,
             Or are you ashamed of him?
Baron: Yes . . . ashamed . . .
Duke: But what did he do?
Baron: He . . . he meant
             To murder me.

The Duke continues with his tactic of taking the Baron's words at face
value:

Duke: Murder! I'll hand him over
             To justice as a foul villain.

This response alarms the Baron, who knows that any investigation
would prove his charge to be unfounded. Unable to withdraw his
words, which would require him to admit openly that he has lied to
his lord, and equally unable to stand by them, he tries to hedge his
statement while still making it as damaging to his son as possible:

Baron: I won't set out to prove it, but I know
             That my death is what he's thirsting for,
             And I know that he's made an attempt
             At . . .
Duke: What?
Baron: Robbing me.

Suddenly the Duke's careful, methodical investigation is shattered by Albert's bursting into the room with the cry, "Baron, you're lying." Up to this point everything has been going in Albert's favor: his father has given such a tangle of implausible, self-contradictory, and obviously stammered excuses that any impartial listener would be inclined to think the Baron must be in the wrong. Whether the hotheaded Albert is capable of recognizing this, or whether he simply is forcing himself to obey the Duke's command, he has managed to keep silent through all his father's lies, even through an accusation of intended murder. But as we have seen, for Albert the fear that his poverty will cause him to be dishonored is an obsession; and the Baron's accusation of attempted theft touches upon exactly this obsession and rouses his son to uncontrollable and even self-destructive fury. Albert's earlier rage at Count Delorge, who had unwittingly touched Albert's fear of poverty-caused dishonor, led him to seek revenge even if he had to risk jousting without a helmet to do it. Now Albert risks the consequences of ignoring his lord's command, rather than allow an accusation relating to the crucial issue of money and honor to go unanswered.

If the Duke's anger at Albert's outburst is predictable, what is surprising is the Baron's response:

> You're here! You dare face me! . . .
> You can say a thing like that to your father! . . .
> I'm lying! and in the presence of our lord! . . .
> To me . . . or am I no longer a knight?

We have already heard this tone of incoherent, white-hot indignation over insulted honor: it is exactly the same tone as Albert's response to Solomon's proposal that he poison his father. Albert is genuinely surprised by Solomon's suggestion; he never bothers to ask whether his own denigration of his father, his openly expressed wish for his father's death, might have encouraged Solomon's line of thought. Albert, in his own self-image, is an honorable man, and an honorable man does not encourage suggestions of parricide; therefore, in Albert's mind, he cannot have encouraged Solomon. The Baron takes this same self-delusional logic even further. The fact that he has no evidence for his accusations against his son — even the fact that the Baron himself does not believe them, or he would have made them at once, instead of first trying a number of obviously flimsy self-justifications — does not stop him from being genuinely furious when his son accuses him of lying. Like Albert, he knows that it is against knightly honor for him to have lied; he still feels that he is a knight; therefore, facts or no facts, whatever he says cannot be a lie. Tragically, he does not realize that the only possible response to his question "Am I no longer a knight?" is "No, not any longer." If there were any doubt on this point, it vanishes when the Baron makes a proposal that any true knight would find as grotesque as it is appalling: a duel with his own son.

Albert, as willing as his father to settle the question of which of these two ambitious men will dominate the other, hastens to pick up the Baron's gauntlet. But at this moment, when both law and common decency are on the point of collapse, the Duke reasserts their authority:

> What did I see? What's this — and in my presence?
> A son accepted the challenge of his old father!
> In what times have I taken upon myself
> The ducal chain! Silence: you, madman,
> And you, tiger cub! Enough.

The Duke pronounces sentence first upon Albert. In his blind passion, Albert has destroyed the very reputation for which he strove so jealously, and thus the Duke's verdict merely confirms what Albert has brought upon himself through his own action: banishment from the court, that is, from the company of honorable and respected knights. The Duke, nevertheless, is not merely incarnate justice: as he turns to the disgraced Baron, he remembers the knight who once, so many years ago, was a small boy's hero, and one can imagine the grief, more than indignation, in his voice, as he quietly asks, "You, unhappy old man, / Are you not ashamed . . ."

But where human justice might pause, a higher justice does not. In challenging his son to a duel, the Baron has explicitly invoked "righteous God," Who, a medieval man would have believed, revealed His judgment in a duel, upholding the innocent and striking down the guilty. The Baron knows how matters must stand for him in such a judgment: by his own admission, he is an oppressor of widows and orphans, a profiteer from robbery and murder. Like Hermann in Pushkin's short story "The Queen of Spades," the Baron is suddenly felled by what can be seen as either a supernatural intervention or the burden of a guilty conscience. Earlier, as he acknowledged the human suffering his treasure represented, the Baron imagined the possibility of "a second Flood" — an act of divine retribution — in which he would die, choking and gasping for air, trapped in his own vault. Now, as he is truly dying, one hears his inability to breathe, his sentences collapsing into gasping fragments:

It's stifling! . . . stifling! . . . Where are the keys?
My keys, keys!

He indeed dies trapped in his vault, not physically but spiritually: in the last moment of his life, when the knight he once was would have thought about repentance or the state of his soul, all the Baron can think about is the gold he has piled up so determinedly and — as is now clear — so futilely. Just as he foresaw, all his ambition has been brought to naught by the one power he acknowledged as greater than his own: mortality.

Confronted with such a consuming passion as the Baron's, the play's voice of reason, the Duke, can do nothing but helplessly exclaim: "A terrible age, terrible hearts!" Yet this single, stunned line carries in it a memorable balance. The "terrible age" echoes the Duke's earlier words, "In what times have I taken upon myself / The ducal chain!"

The force that has dishonored Albert and destroyed the Baron—the desire for wealth and reputation without a character worthy of them, leading in its logical extreme to the demand for power without any moral limitations—is recognized as not just an individual corruption, but a social one. Nevertheless, the Duke does not regard human beings as the passive victims of society, helpless to resist the constraints of circumstance. The Baron has the freedom to choose his actions, and he uses that freedom to make choices that destroyed his own better nature—the choices of a "terrible heart." The essential power of the "little tragedies," the source of their ability to evoke grief as well as horror, lies in precisely that recognition: each play is the story of a great and gifted figure who could avoid his own self-ruin, and who instead freely chooses it.

Betrayal of a Calling: *Mozart and Salieri*

THE PLOT OF *Mozart and Salieri* was suggested to Pushkin by a persistent though unfounded rumor that Mozart died as the result of poison administered by a rival composer, Antonio Salieri. In an undated note, apparently from 1832, Pushkin wrote: "At the premiere of *Don Giovanni*, when the whole theater, filled with astounded music lovers, was hushed, intoxicated by Mozart's harmonies, a whistle [of derision] was heard—everyone turned in indignation, and the celebrated Salieri stalked out of the hall—in a fury, consumed by envy. . . . The envier who could whistle at *Don Giovanni* could poison its creator."[1] This note suggests that Pushkin's belief in Salieri's guilt was not so much the approach of a historian as that of a psychological novelist. Yet this point of view presents its own challenge. From his own position in the literary world, Pushkin knew all too well the envy and hatred that genius can arouse in a hack. But Salieri was no hack; he was one of the most prominent composers of his day, a man of sufficient artistic stature that such librettists as Da Ponte (Mozart's librettist for both *Le nozze di Figaro* and *Don Giovanni*) and Beaumarchais were willing to work with him. How could such a composer, a man for whom music was one of the most important things in his life, bring himself to murder one of the greatest figures in the history of European music? How would he perceive and justify such an action, and how would it affect him? These are the questions underlying *Mozart and Salieri.*

From the play's opening, Salieri appears as an isolated figure, at odds not only with the conventional wisdom of his world, but with the universe itself, as he speaks three of the most explosive lines with which any drama has ever opened:

> They say there's no justice here on earth,
> But there's no justice higher up, either. To me
> That's as clear and simple as do-re-mi.

Spoken by a man of the eighteenth century, such words evoke the challenge to God of the radical Enlightenment. However, these words are born, not from the study of philosophy or society or history, but from the torment of a life divided against itself, a life story he pours out in his monologue. From Salieri's point of view, he is presenting a massive indictment against Heaven itself. But from an outsider's point of view, he is chronicling an inner struggle between an artistic vocation and an ambition destructive to that vocation. Of the vocation itself, Salieri allows no doubt:

> I was born with a love for art;
> When I was a child, when up on high
> The organ's notes echoed in our old church,

I listened and was spellbound — I wept,
Sweet tears flowed against my will.

From those tears a passion for music is born, a passion which, like
a jealous love, excludes everything else from Salieri's life:

Early I refused all idle amusements;
To know anything other than music was
Hateful to me; stubbornly and proudly
I denied all else and gave myself up
To music alone.

Yet, though he speaks of "love of art," the tone of Salieri's words is
not loving but defensive, wrathful. One feels that he sees himself as
a sort of lonely Old Testament prophet whose faithfulness to his one
true God — music — is constantly being assailed by the idolaters surrounding him. What temptation is it that he is resisting so firmly? He
tells us of his trials:

The first steps were hard
And the first path was tedious. I overcame
My early difficulties. I gave craft
Its place as the foundation stone of art;
I made myself a craftsman; my fingers
Acquired obedient, cold dexterity
And my ear, accuracy. I killed sounds,
Dissected music like a corpse. I put harmony
To the test of algebra.

Bizarre as it seems, the temptation, the obstacle in Salieri's way, is —
Salieri. As the images of dissection and mathematics remind us, Salieri
is indeed a man of the Enlightenment, a man of reason. Creativity, he

is convinced, must have rules, natural laws, no less than biology or chemistry. All he has to do is to discover the laws, to understand how they work, and then he can apply them; then he will be the musician he dreams of being. But in concentrating so exclusively on what is accessible to reason, on method and system, Salieri is doing violence to the very emotion that first made him a musician, the irrational impulse that expressed itself in his childhood tears. It is this determination to gain power by subjecting living intuition to the dead hand of an all-encompassing system that gives Salieri his spiritual kinship with such Dostoevskian heroes as Raskolnikov and Ivan Karamazov, a kinship pointed out by Rassadin.[2] And just how far Salieri is willing to go in such subjection he makes terrifyingly clear:

> Often, after sitting silently in my cell
> Two or three days, forgetting sleep and food,
> After the taste of ecstasy and tears of inspiration,
> I burned my work and watched coldly
> As my idea and the sounds I had brought forth
> Blazed up, then vanished with a puff of smoke.

Here we see the two Salieris, the child overcome by beauty and the determined master of the system, at war with each other. Neither Salieri is a stranger to sacrifice, but for the first one, sacrifice is not a conscious, painful gritting of teeth, but something he does willingly, even unconsciously: he "forgets" to eat and sleep, so caught up is he in his inspiration. The work is so intimately a part of his being that he speaks, not merely of the sounds he created, but the sounds he "brought forth" — to which he gave birth. Whether in the eyes of a critic his work is a good one or is flawed, or whether after another twenty years of experience and development Salieri himself would regard it as good or flawed, is at that moment irrelevant. What is important is that Salieri himself realizes that he has expressed the idea he loves, his inspiration, as best he can within the limits of his experience and ability. He has given himself completely. And in response, how does the "other" Salieri treat this work? "I burned my work and watched coldly . . ." One would have thought that if Salieri had wept to hear the church organ, he would have wept tears of blood to see his work destroyed. Instead he "watched coldly"—as if it were not even his. In the view of his relentless logic, this early work was merely the experiment of a beginner, "not daring yet even to think of glory," and as such has no right to survive. How its creator happens to feel about his own work is completely beside the point:

> . . .When the great Gluck
> Appeared and revealed to us new mysteries
> (Deep and captivating mysteries),
> Didn't I abandon everything I'd known before,
> Everything I'd loved and believed so fervently,
> And didn't I set out boldly after him
> Without a murmur, like one who's lost his path
> And is directed to go another way?

Unexpectedly, the two Salieris, the Salieri of the artistic impulse and the Salieri of the system, seem to enter into an unlikely alliance. It is Salieri the artist who humbly recognizes Gluck as a greater artist than himself, the revealer of "deep and captivating mysteries." But it is Salieri the rationalist who seizes on this recognition and deduces from it that the path to glory is simply to follow in Gluck's footsteps. Ironically, if Salieri could have carried out this plan, it would have been a failure even in a purely careerist sense: why should the public want a copy of Gluck, when it already had the original? It has been said that the rule for a successful sequel is that it should be like the original, but different. In the same way, one suspects that the source of Salieri's success is precisely that while deliberately imitating composers greater than himself, he is still enough of an artist that he unconsciously introduces some touch of his own inspiration. Salieri himself, of course, does not realize this. Rather, he sees everything that he achieves as merely what he has earned through his work and study:

> By concentrated, constant effort
> Finally in the unbounded realm of art
> I achieved a high place. Glory
> Smiled on me; in people's hearts
> I found the harmonies that I'd created.
> I was happy . . .

At this stage, as Salieri points out, he feels no resentment toward his more successful colleagues. He sees them as living in the same type of world, operating under the same sort of rules, as he does; he has every confidence that with more effort, more study, greater mastery, he can hope to equal them. Indeed, Salieri indignantly repudiates the very idea that he could envy Gluck or Piccini on the grounds that such envy would be an insult to his own abilities and dignity:

> No! I never once felt envy then,
> No, never! — not even when Piccini
> Learned to charm the savage Paris audience,
> Not even when I heard for the first time
> The opening chords of *Iphigenia*.
> Who will say that proud Salieri
> Was ever a contemptible envier,
> A snake trodden powerless underfoot,
> Left half-alive to bite the dirt and dust?

The full magnitude of Salieri's ambition, and thus the depth of his horror at the thought of its failure, is revealed in the extraordinarily forcefulness and detail of the metaphor he uses to depict his humiliation. Surely it is no accident that, in the image of the serpent, he evokes the downfall of the greatest of all ambitions — that of Lucifer himself.[3]

But now, for the first time, Salieri is forced into the humiliating confession that there is someone he envies, someone who he realizes can do what he cannot. As he sees it, everything which he has worked so hard for, everything which he should have rightfully earned, has unfairly been given to another who did nothing to deserve it. Just as the Baron in *The Miserly Knight* cries out at the thought of his treasure being inherited by his idle son:

> No, first suffer through piling up your own wealth,
> And then let's see if some unhappy man
> Will come and squander what you got by blood . . .

so too Salieri is infuriated at the thought that the idler Mozart has acquired with no effort the treasure he himself most desires:

> . . . But now — I say it myself — now
> I am an envier. I feel envy; deep,
> Tormenting envy. Oh heaven!
> Where is rightness, when the sacred gift,
> Immortal genius, comes not as reward
> For ardent love and self-renunciation,
> Labor, zeal, diligence, and prayers —
> But bestows its radiant halo on a madman
> Who idly strolls through life? Oh, Mozart, Mozart!

And it is just at this moment, as Salieri confesses his own baffled, furious, impotent humiliation, that he hears a familiar voice: "Aha! You saw me! And I wanted / To give you a surprise amusement." Mozart, hearing his name spoken, has completely misunderstood Salieri's motive. He believes that Salieri sees him, is addressing him in greeting, whereas exactly the reverse is the case: Salieri would never have said such words as he had just spoken if he knew that his rival were there. One can imagine Salieri turning with a start and blurting out:

"You're here!—When'd you get here?" He could not be less interested in Mozart's "surprise" or even his presence, except to try to find the answer to a question he does not dare put directly: how much of that humiliating confession did you overhear?

Such verbal cross-purposes, such a failure on the part of each man to grasp or correctly predict the response of the other, characterizes the interchanges of Mozart and Salieri throughout the scene. Mozart's "surprise"—the performance of the blind fiddler—arouses in Salieri, not the laughter Mozart expected, but indignation. Mozart's own performance, coming on the heels of what Salieri regards as his display of vulgarity, then astounds—and appalls—Salieri:

> You were coming to me with that
> And you could stop off at a tavern
> And listen to a blind fiddler!—My God!

And the ecstatic praises of Mozart with which Salieri follows this exclamation are clearly not what Mozart himself expected, as shown by the awkwardness of his reply: "Bah! really? well, maybe . . ." It is as if the two men are speaking not to but past each other, engaged in a dialogue of the deaf.

Through these constant failures to find a common language, the crucial differences in the two men's understanding of art are revealed. Salieri's response to the unintended parody resulting from the blind fiddler's inept performance is not simply an expression of dislike for entertainment geared to the low taste of the crowd. The real source of Salieri's anger, as will become clear in his second monologue, is that he sees art much as the Baron sees his gold—as a treasure to be guarded, kept from desecration by irreverent or prodigal hands, whether the threat to it is as trivial as the one posed by a poor blind fiddler, or as great as the one that, in Salieri's opinion, Mozart himself represents. For Mozart, by contrast, art can be freely "spent"; there is no danger that it will be used up, or that the value it contains will be lost or debased. He is not the guardian of art, because he knows that art needs no guardian: that after the inept, the vulgar, and the mercenary have done their worst, art will still remain. And with this consciousness, he can afford to laugh at an unintended parody.

But Mozart's laughter goes deeper than this, as shown by his description of the piece he plays for Salieri:

> Imagine someone—who?
> Well, say myself—only a little younger—
> In love—not all that deeply, but a little—
> I'm with a pretty girl, or with a friend—say you,
> I'm in good spirits—Just then a ghostly vision,
> A sudden gloom, or something of that sort . . .

In light of the second scene of the play, we realize that these words of Mozart's describe precisely the position he himself is in at the moment he speaks them. The gaiety of his past—the time when he was "a little younger"—already draws to its end; his path has been crossed by a dark shadow, "a ghostly vision." The black man has already come to his house, the *Requiem* has already been commissioned. And so, as Mozart passes the tavern, as he hears the music he created in his earlier days of joy, as he is greeted by the noise and the laughter of the crowd, he feels the irresistible urge to participate in that gaiety one last time: "This thou perceiv'st which makes thy love more strong, / To love that well which thou must leave ere long." Mozart's laughter at that moment is a laughter of farewell. What the blind fiddler's playing means to Mozart at that moment cannot be conveyed to Salieri, not only because of Salieri's own limitations, but because a mere reproduction of that playing would not convey to anyone the significance it assumes for Mozart. That significance comes through only in Mozart's own work. And Salieri the artist, to his credit, recognizes that he has heard something extraordinary:

What depth!
What boldness and what just proportion!
You, Mozart, are a god, and you yourself don't know it . . .

"You are a god": these words again underscore the gulf between Mozart and Salieri. The image of the artist as inspired by a god, or as the servant of a god, is one of the oldest ideas in Western art. Pushkin paid his own tribute to it in several works, notably the poem "The Poet" ("Пока не требует поэта . . ."). But for Pushkin, the glory belongs to the god and not to the servant. Indeed, when the servant is not being guided by the god, he may be not merely no greater than others, but even inferior to them ("И меж детей ничтожных мира, / Быть может, всех ничтожней он"). For Salieri, the artist is himself a god rather than a man, let alone an unworthy man (ничтожный). In place of Heaven (which has proven to be "unjust" and is thus discredited), Salieri, the man of the Enlightenment, puts man's own will, dependent on no outside inspiration, relying on its own resources to scale the heights. So vast a claim disconcerts Mozart, who promptly disowns it by pointing to his own all-too-human limitations: "my divineness is hungry."

One can only imagine what humiliation "proud Salieri" must suffer at that moment: it is painful enough that, carried away for an instant by his own rapture, he has involuntarily given his rival such an accolade as he has dreamed of all his adult life, and dreamed of in vain; but how much more painful it must be that that rival, in return, brushes the prize aside as if it were nothing. In that instant, the plot forms in Salieri's mind: "Listen, let's have dinner together . . ." And as soon as Mozart is out of earshot, Salieri immediately tries to overcome his humiliation by an impassioned assertion that he, too, possesses a role of enormous significance, indeed, that he is the chosen one of history:

No! I cannot set myself against
My destiny — I am the one who's chosen

To stop him — or else we all will perish,
All of us, priests and servitors of music,
Not only myself with my empty glory . . .

This outburst marks a fatal shift in Salieri's hostility toward Mozart. Before, Salieri only complained of the "unfairness" of Mozart's getting for free what he, Salieri, had to put in years of labor to achieve. Now Salieri fully realizes that there is no way that he can ever equal Mozart's achievements. Mozart is simply too great a phenomenon to be caught within the meshes of Salieri's system: what Mozart does, no matter how much one analyzes it, still has a mystery at the core; it will never be fully graspable and reproducible. It cannot be harnessed and put to use by other musicians — and what is not useful, for Salieri's Enlightenment mentality, has no right to exist. Further, since Salieri has come to identify his system with art itself, that means that Mozart is not an artist, but rather a force outside of art, even hostile to art:

What is the use if Mozart lives
And even achieves still greater heights?
What he does — will he elevate Art? No,
It will fall again when he has vanished;
No heir of his will remain among us.
What use is he? Appearing like an angel,
He brings us a few of Heaven's songs,
And then, once he's roused a wingless desire
In us, children of dust, he flies away!
Fly away then! And the sooner, the better!

Even now, as Salieri contemplates Mozart's death, Salieri's own artistic nature, his irresistible love for Mozart, still comes through: he sees Mozart as no less than an angel, bringing the music of Heaven itself to mere mortals. Such words give one a glimpse of what the relationship between Mozart and Salieri could have been. Pushkin's Mozart, after all, is neither an angel nor a saint of the wilderness: he is a man very much engaged in the lives of those around him, a man who stops in at taverns, who tells his wife not to expect him for supper, who plays on the floor with his little boy. So much has been said about the dangers of Salieri's asceticism, its risk of losing touch with human reality, that it takes an effort to realize that Mozart's sociability also has a potential vulnerability: with so much of his life committed to people who like or even love him, but who as nonmusicians are incapable of appreciating the importance of his art, he himself is in danger of having his views colored by theirs, of trivializing his work, of treating it as merely a pleasant diversion or a way to make money. This is one temptation to which Salieri is immune: with his impassioned, even violent response to music, he cannot accept an art of anything less than maximal expressiveness. His greatest term of praise is "depth": he admires Gluck for revealing "deep and captivating mysteries"; the first ecstatic words he utters about Mozart's work are, "What depth! What boldness!" and only after that, as a secondary merit, does he note the work's Classicism—"what just proportion!" Mozart recognizes Salieri's uncompromising, maximalist approach to art: that is why he trusts Salieri's artistic judgment more than his own, why after sketching out his ideas he comes to Salieri to ask if they are good. Salieri's artistic nature needs Mozart, but Mozart also needs Salieri—not as a composer, but as a listener. The tragedy is that to Salieri in his pride the role of listener appears a contemptibly secondary one: the angelic music arouses in him not simply joy and gratitude but "wingless desire" — the desire himself to ascend Heaven, a desire which he knows cannot be gratified. And if it cannot, then let even the joy of the music be gone, so long as the torment of unfulfillable ambition is relieved:

Fly away then! And the sooner the better!

Here is the poison, my Izora's final gift . . .

What a profoundly disturbing image: this never-explained Izora, seemingly the only human being whom the isolated Salieri loved not for art's sake but simply for herself, and the last gift she gave him was—poison. Whoever she was, however they parted, she seems to have understood him all too well. For Salieri's consuming ambition has itself proved to be a poison, one which has destroyed both his own inner peace and his relations with others, so that it seems to him that it would be a small step to complete physically the ruin that has already occurred spiritually. But just as in his first monologue Salieri boasts of the self-mastery he showed in his study of music, so again he takes pride in the self-mastery that stopped him from using the poison:

> For eighteen years I've carried it with me—
> And often in that time I have found life
> An unbearable wound, and often I have sat
> At table with a heedless enemy.
> And, yes, I heard the whisper of temptation
> But I didn't yield, although I am no coward,
> Although I feel an injury deeply,
> Although I love life little. Still I waited.

And then, utterly unexpectedly, like Ivan Karamazov, ferocious, embittered, believing in nothing and yet still passionately loving the "the sticky little green leaves," Salieri suddenly remembers his love of music:

> When the thirst for death tormented me,
> Why die? —I thought: it may be, life
> Will bring me unexpected gifts;
> Rapture, it may be, will come to me
> In a creative night of inspiration;
> It may be some new Haydn will bring forth
> Greatness—and I will rejoice in it . . .

But just as suddenly as the radiance appears, it disappears, darkened by Salieri's destructive pride. The same repeated "it may be" that had been a phrase of hope and inspiration now becomes only a threat of yet greater humiliation, and thus greater agony. And if Salieri is not to be the powerless serpent of his first monologue, helplessly trodden in the dust, he must at least retain the ability to revenge himself on his tormentor:

> When I feasted with a hated guest,
> It may be—I thought—a still worse foe
> Awaits me; an injury still worse, it may be,
> Will strike me down from some proud height—
> Then you won't be in vain, Izora's gift.

But from Salieri's point of view, there could be no injury worse than to threaten to overthrow his system, on which he rests his hopes of becoming a great musician. The one time when either his pride must be destroyed, or he must use his long-hoarded weapon, is at hand:

> And I was right! At last I've found
> My enemy, and at last a new Haydn
> Wondrously has enraptured me!
> Now it's time! cherished gift of love,
> For you to go today into friendship's cup.

Throughout the monologue Salieri's determination to kill Mozart has been clear, but these lines introduce an additional possibility: a murder-suicide. The hope of finding a new Haydn, after all, is what has prevented Salieri from killing himself. Now that that hope has been fulfilled—only to be lost soon, once and for all, by Mozart's death—Salieri's own motive for continuing to live collapses. And, as V. Vatsuro points out, in Pushkin's lyric poems, the terms "the friendly cup" (чаша дружеская) and "the round-robin cup" (чаша круговая) are used interchangeably to refer to a custom by which, as a gesture of friendship, a single cup would be passed around the table for everyone to drink from in turn; and while the more natural place for this custom would be at a full-scale banquet, it could also be observed by only two people.[4] This possibility of suicide is so obliquely stated, in contrast to the brutal directness of the plot against Mozart, that Salieri might not consciously be aware of it. Nevertheless, Salieri's language clearly reflects his realization, if only subconscious, that Mozart's life and his own existence as an artist are interrelated, that to destroy one in the name of his system is also to destroy the other.

The second scene, in the tavern, opens with what appears to be a reversal of the roles of Mozart and Salieri: it is Salieri the ascetic who praises the food and particularly the wine; it is Mozart who disregards them. Instead, Mozart is preoccupied—not primarily with his own impending death, although he is acutely aware of that, but with his last creative effort, his final and greatest artistic ascent. From the very moment when he hears that an unknown man has come to his house and asked for him, Mozart senses that this is a turning point in his fate, and lies awake anxiously wondering what it means: "But all night I thought: who could it be? / And what was I to him?" And yet when Mozart actually meets this ominous figure, and is told that there is still an artistic task for him to perform, Mozart does not allow himself any further anxiety, but immediately gives himself up to his work:

I went out. A man dressed all in black
Greeted me respectfully, ordered from me
A requiem, and vanished. I sat down
And began to write at once . . .

All of this happened "three weeks ago"—before Salieri had formed his murderous intent. And suddenly we realize that Salieri, who is so confident that it is his decision, his will, that controls the course of events, is in fact merely an agent. Behind him, allowing him to act, stands Fate. The same Higher Will that inexplicably granted Mozart his supreme artistry (unjustly, Salieri would say) is now just as inexplicably setting a term to his life. And Mozart recognizes it:

> . . . since then
> My black man's never come back to my house;
> And I'm glad; I'd hate to have to part
> With my work, although the *Requiem*
> Already is complete . . .

Why does Mozart speak of parting with his work? After all, he is not in the position of a painter or sculptor, who must physically part with their own creations. What a composer or a writer produces is an idea, which he does not lose simply because it is then written down; as the bookseller in Pushkin's "A Bookseller Talking with a Poet" ("Разговор книгопродавца с поэтом") points out, selling your manuscript doesn't mean selling your inspiration. Mozart is parting with his work because the *Requiem* was his last work not just chronologically, but teleologically: all that he was called upon to do in his lifetime is now finished, and he knows it. Hence the apparent inconsistency of Mozart's referring to the *Requiem* as "complete," whereas in fact the *Requiem* is not complete, and was finished by Mozart's pupil Süssmayr. In Pushkin's mythological rather than historical approach, the *Requiem* is complete because it ought to be complete; the fact is adjusted to fit what for Pushkin is the greater truth—that the artist dies not at a random moment, not because of the spite of lesser men or because of casual events which could equally well have happened differently, but because the moment of Fate arrives: his work is done, his time has come. And Mozart accepts this with the same humility with which he accepted his gift itself: although he speaks of being continuously followed by the black man, he never expresses fear of this man. Such a feeling is merely ascribed to him by Salieri, in a typical misunderstanding:

> . . . What childish fear is this?
> Drop this useless brooding. Beaumarchais
> Used to tell me, "Brother Salieri, listen;
> When black thoughts come to trouble you,
> Pop the cork on a bottle of champagne,
> Or reread *The Marriage of Figaro.*"

After the simplicity and truthfulness of Mozart's words, this speech has so false a ring as to be grating: can one really imagine Salieri popping the cork on a bottle of champagne? Salieri's motive is all too clear: incapable of understanding the spiritual process going on within Mozart, but aware that Mozart is conscious that death is near, Salieri can only assume that his intended victim has somehow become suspicious. So Salieri tries to distract those suspicions, to say something he thinks will appeal to the man whom he has described as "idly strolling through life." And for a moment, Salieri's words do indeed call back Mozart's memory of his past life. But that memory is almost immediately overwhelmed by his acute consciousness of the present fateful moment, so that his thoughts abruptly shift from merriment to an agonized question:

> Good! Beaumarchais was after all your friend;
> You wrote the music for his *Tarara,*
> A splendid thing. There's a motif in it . . .
> I always think of it when I am happy . . .
> La la la la. . . . Ah, is it true, Salieri,
> That Beaumarchais poisoned someone?

Salieri's answer, "I don't think so; he was too much a buffoon / For such a craft," suggests that he, like Raskolnikov, is suddenly overcome by the temptation to say something pointing to his own guilt at the very moment when his conscious plan was to try to look innocent. For if a good sense of humor makes one unqualified to be a poisoner, then

Salieri conversely would certainly seem to be well qualified for the job; and Salieri's description of poisoning as a "craft" (ремесло) suggests his earlier description of himself as a "craftsman" (ремесленник). Yet Mozart ignores these warning signs—not simply because of his naive trustfulness, as some critics have asserted, but because he is preoccupied with a much larger question, one that Salieri has not addressed. He is not merely asking whether a specific individual, Beaumarchais, committed a great crime, but whether it is possible for a genuinely inspired figure—whether Beaumarchais, or Salieri, or himself—to commit a great crime. And he comes to the conclusion that it is not:

> He's a genius,
> Like you and me. And genius and crime
> Are two things that don't combine. Isn't that true?

With these words, Mozart is able to face death with equanimity: his life has been well spent. Pushkin, looking back on his own life in "My Own Monument I've Built, Not Made by Any Hand" ("Я памятник себе воздвиг нерукотворный"), would one day sum up his artistic achievement in moral terms:

> И долго буду тем любезен я народу,
> Что чувства добрые я лирой пробуждал,
> Что в мой жестокий век восславил я Свободу
>   И милость к падшим призывал.

> [My memory will be loved among the people long,
> Because kind feelings were by my lyre awakened,
> Because in my cruel age, I praised Freedom in my song
>   And mercy to those forsaken.]

Similarly, Mozart, approaching death and looking back on his life, is able to say that he has been a true artist, and thus on the side of right.

For whatever the individual faults of an artist may have been, art itself has always sought harmony and meaning even in life's terrors and cruelties, has always pointed to something crucial to human life that is above mere greed and selfishness.

Such an opposition between art and self-aggrandizement is a clear if unintended challenge to Salieri, for whom art has become precisely his form of asserting supremacy. And he takes up the challenge:

> You think so?
> (*Pours the poison into Mozart's glass.*)
> Well then, drink.

Salieri is inviting Mozart to stake his life on his beliefs: for if (as Mozart has said) Salieri is a genius, and if "genius and crime / Are two things that don't combine," then Mozart would be able to drink in complete safety. The aggressiveness of Salieri's response is emphasized by Pushkin's stage direction, "Бросает яд" — "throws the poison" or "flings the poison" — something that is difficult to envision being performed literally, but that at least emphasizes that Salieri's gesture has none of the furtiveness that one might expect of a poisoner, but is performed boldly, in a barely concealed manner. And Mozart takes up the invitation unhesitatingly: he lifts the glass and pronounces a toast:

> To your
> Health, my friend, and to the faithful union
> That binds together Mozart and Salieri,
> Two sons of harmony.

The irony of the victim extolling his friendship with his murderer, the contrast between the generosity of the one and the malignance of the other, is already so great as to be almost unbearable. Yet what follows it is far more wrenching: Mozart gives one of the most extraordinary privileges in the history of music — the honor of being an audience of one at his last performance, which is also the only performance he will ever give of his *Requiem*—to the very man who has vowed to stop him from creating any more music. Again, it must be repeated that this intensely tragic situation is not merely the result of naivete on Mozart's part. The Salieri to whom he is speaking and for whom he is playing, the Salieri whom he ranks with Beaumarchais and himself as a genius, even (who would have thought it?) the Salieri whose tune Mozart regularly thinks of *when he is happy*—this Salieri, Salieri the artist, has as real an existence as Salieri the brooding, ambitious rationalist-murderer. Indeed, the struggle between the two Salieris is at that moment so evenly matched that at the crucial moment, as Mozart lifts the cup to drink, Salieri almost aborts the very crime he has so carefully planned, crying out, "Stop, stop, stop!" In so terse a play, such a threefold repetition underscores its significance. There is only one way that line could be delivered: in an outburst of uncontrollable agony. But the deed is done, Salieri sees that his outcry has affected nothing, and he gives a terrible sigh of mixed horror and relief: "You drank it." And then he remembers his earlier plan to escape his own horror at his deed, by using "friendship's cup" for not merely a murder but a murder-suicide, and realizes that even that escape from his own inner strife is no longer open to him. Mozart has defied his expectations and thwarted him one last time; and he can only add reproachfully: ". . . without me?"

But there are a few moments left before he will truly be "without" Mozart, for there is still the performance of the *Requiem*. Amid the terrible disharmony of his own soul, Salieri still tries to cling to this last one of "Heaven's songs," this last vision of harmony:

> These tears
> Are the first I've shed—from pain and pleasure,
> As if I had fulfilled a burdening duty,
> As if the surgeon's knife had cut from me
> The part that suffered! Friend Mozart, these tears . . .

Don't notice them. Continue, still make haste
To fill my soul with sounds . . .

Salieri's agony and relief spring from the same cause: that the rationalist, the master of the system, the murderer, within him has finally
gained a decisive victory over the artist within—a relief because it
finally ends his inner strife, but an agony because part of himself has
been destroyed. Thus he speaks of his tears at that moment as his first:
his earlier tears as a child, at the moment of discovering his artistic
vocation, have been obliterated from his memory, just as that vocation itself has been crushed in his soul. From Salieri's early destruction of his beloved first works, to his abandonment of "everything I'd
known before, / Everything I'd loved and believed so fervently" when
he became a disciple of Gluck, to his poisoning the very composer
whom he loves above all others and hails as the "new Haydn"—it all
forms a single trajectory, which finally reaches its logical end: spiritual
self-destruction. Salieri may plead for the music to go on; but Mozart
answers his plea with words, not with continued playing. Music as a
source of meaning, of spiritual life, for Salieri has come to an end.

Struck by Salieri's emotion, Mozart replies:

If only everyone could feel the power
Of harmony like you! but no, for then
The world could not exist; no one would want
To spend time taking care of life's low needs;
All would be given over to free art.
We are but few, we chosen, happy idlers
Who look disdainfully at petty usefulness
And form a priesthood serving only beauty.
Isn't that so?

This speech has been disdained by critics as conventional and unin-
spired. It is true that if it were a freestanding lyric rather than part

of a drama, it would be close to the gratingly superior tone that mars such Pushkinian lyrics as "To the Poet" ("Поет! не дорожи любовию народой . . .") or "The Poet and the Crowd" ("Поет и толпа"). The force of this speech comes from its context, as a response to Salieri's passionate outcry, and as an outcry itself, though less passionate than wistful: "If only everyone could feel the power . . ." These are unmistakably the words of a man who knows what it is to suffer estrangement from others. We are accustomed to thinking of Mozart as an easily accessible composer, and indeed there are arias of his which could be (and probably have been) played by a fiddler in a tavern. But we forget that a number of his compositions simply overwhelmed his contemporaries, and were admired by only the cognoscenti. Pushkin's Mozart— like Pushkin himself—knew what it was to put his heart into a work and to find no sympathetic audience. Mozart can tell himself that most people spend most of their time on the business of making a living and thus cannot be expected to appreciate music as an artist does, or that his isolation is a form of honor, marking him as one of the chosen few. But these words fail to have power precisely because they are attempts to deal rationally, logically, with a spontaneously arising need for spiritual kinship, a need so strong that after delivering these proudly independent and even dogmatic sentences, Mozart immediately seeks his interlocutor's agreement, adding, "Isn't that so?"

Mozart's willingness to appeal to Salieri as an equal, as a man who can understand him, makes one realize not merely how terrible Salieri's crime is, but, from Mozart's point of view, how inexplicable, how tragically unnecessary. "If only everyone could feel the power . . ." For Mozart, artistry or nonartistry reduces itself to a single issue: the depth and commitment of one's response to beauty. The whole question of artistic ranking, of superiority and inferiority, that obsesses Salieri means nothing to Mozart. If one could imagine Mozart and Salieri with the same personalities, but with their degrees of musical ability reversed, not only would a musically inferior Mozart not murder a musically superior Salieri, but the very idea that such a superiority was a painful humiliation to others would not cross the lesser musician's mind. To "feel the power of harmony" strongly enough, to respond to and create as much beauty as one can, with as much skill and love as one can bring to the work — it is that, not one's specific level of achievements, which in Mozart's view makes one an artist.

For Mozart, as for Salieri, to be an artist is to be part of a priesthood. But one enters this priesthood not, as Salieri imagines, through the merit of one's own hard work (indeed, the real hard work is done by those "taking care of life's low needs," in whose eyes artists are privileged "idlers"). Rather, this "priestly" status comes from the choice one makes: to love beauty more or to love something else more, something else that falls under the general heading "usefulness" (польза). For the crowd in "The Poet and the Crowd," the "usefulness" (польза) they demand is moral instruction. In another context, one could easily imagine an economic benefit as being the criterion of "usefulness" that is to be preferred to beauty. For Salieri, "usefulness" implies suitability for incorporation into a musical tradition that can be studied and emulated, and the recognition that Mozart's music is inimitable leads him to ask, "What is the use (пользы) if Mozart lives. . . . What use is he?" The important point is not what specific goal is understood as "useful," but rather what choice will be made when this goal comes into conflict with the desire for beauty; for no one can serve two masters. Only those who are willing steadfastly to reject other goals and serve beauty first are true members of the "priesthood" — a demand stern enough, Mozart realizes, that few will be able to achieve it. One might have thought that if anyone could achieve it, it would be the ascetic, single-minded Salieri. But one who feels little attraction to the petty sins of the flesh may be all the more vulnerable to the sins of the mind and spirit, to ambition and envy. To these great sins has Salieri fallen prey, while Mozart, despite his willingness to trifle with distractions that Salieri would never have noticed, nevertheless could say that he had never seriously allowed them to interfere with his art—a fact which even Salieri would admit. Mozart has been faithful literally unto death; and now, having completed and performed what he knows is his final work, at last he is overcome by the exhaustion of his last effort and the ever-increasing nearness of death:

> But now I feel unwell,
> Something weighs me down; I want to sleep.
> Farewell!

This final line (in Russian, прощай же) is extraordinary. In keeping with Mozart's recognition of his own impending fate, it is not the ordinary "good-bye" one would use with a person whom one expected to see again in the normal course of events; it is used only when one expects a prolonged separation, perhaps a permanent one. But more than that, it has a secondary meaning of "forgive me." The victim, having finished all the other tasks remaining to him on earth, performs a last one—he asks forgiveness of his own murderer.

Against this final act of humility Salieri hardens his heart. Rather than answer in the same way, he replies with a conventional good-bye—"Until we meet again" (До свиданья). His response is purely that of the murderer pretending that nothing is amiss, automatically lying lest the smallest detail betray him. He has understood so little of all that Mozart has said to him that he still regards Mozart's intuitive precognition of death merely as a suspicion of him that he must disarm. One can almost hear his malicious sign of relief and pleasure at (as he thinks) having successfully gulled his victim, as he says after Mozart's departure, "You will sleep / A long time, Mozart!"

But one thing Mozart said has penetrated, and disturbs Salieri:

> But is he really right
> And am I not a genius? Genius and crime
> Are two things that don't combine.

He quickly reaches for a rationalization—"That's not true: / What of Michelangelo?"—recalling a legend that Michelangelo had killed a man in order to observe the appropriate expression for a painting of the dying Christ. But at the very moment he offers this excuse, Salieri himself suspects its flimsiness: "or is that just a fable / Of the stupid, senseless crowd (толпы) . . . ?"

To be one of the "crowd," not to be a genius—this, for Salieri, is a fate worse than death. But the means on which Salieri counted to raise himself above the crowd—the pursuit of a musical "system" and his willingness to sacrifice anything, or anyone, threatening it—proves to be precisely what brings him down to the crowd's level. The logical implication of Mozart's final speech is that Salieri's hostility toward the artist-"idler" and his preference for "usefulness" rather than beauty put him on the side of the "senseless crowd" rather than that of the artist. Salieri himself, in his final lines, begins to recognize this similarity: he has accepted a story that Mozart would immediately have rejected (as he rejected the story of Beaumarchais the poisoner), and that only the crowd would believe.

Salieri did not drink from the poisoned cup. Nevertheless, he has committed a murder-suicide, not physically but spiritually. In destroying Mozart, he has also destroyed his own artistic self, the source of his inner power. Ahead of him there still lies a long life—but a life of empty years, devoid of meaning, its core shattered. Genius and crime have indeed proven to be two things that don't combine—and by his actions Salieri has made his choice once and for all between them.

The Weight of the Past: *The Stone Guest*

THE STONE GUEST has aroused far more controversy, expressed in more extreme terms, than any other of Pushkin's dramatic works. As if to echo Doña Anna's question to Don Juan—"Who knows you?"—radically different interpretations of his character have been offered. For Blagoy, Don Juan is a "Mozartean" figure, radiant and life-loving, boldly challenging the gloomy, death-haunted world of medieval Spain:

> Living, turbulent, triumphant life, personified in the figure
> of Don Juan, is constantly overshadowed by a "gloomy vision"
> —the persistently arising specter of death. . . . But life not
> only constantly appears in the play side by side with death.

Life issues a challenge to death . . . especially in Don Juan's
invitation to the statue of the knight-commander to guard his
rendezvous with Doña Anna. And throughout the play life
triumphs. Only at the very end does death prove to be the
victor, and even then, as in Mozart's opera, it does not have
the power to break Don Juan's spirit.[1]

Ustyuzhanin similarly asserts: "The dead and soulless world could not
forgive Don Juan precisely for his live human feeling. . . . The Baron
[in *The Miserly Knight*] perished because he had *ceased* to be a human
being; the same 'iron age' avenges itself on Don Juan because the human being in him had *awakened*."[2] Rassadin, in his study of Pushkin's
plays, gave the chapter on *The Stone Guest* the blunt title "Punishment Without Crime."[3] All three critics take it for granted that Don
Juan's profession of a special love for Doña Anna is indeed truthful.
By contrast, Seeley sees Don Juan as "a mixture of child-like artist and
perverse, compulsive neurotic" who is characterized by a "headlong
pursuit of his own ends in total disregard of the feelings and inter-
ests of others" and argues that Don Juan's pursuit of Doña Anna is,
in fact, just one more seduction.[4] Gregg sees Don Juan as being "in
the process of falling sincerely, even virtuously, in love" with Doña
Anna and regards Don Juan's challenge to the statue as motivated
principally by a lover's jealousy, but adds, "Insolence, cruelty, and a
desire for self-punishment may also be involved."[5] Nepomnyashchy,
while conceding that Don Juan is "charming . . . spontaneous as a
child . . . talented [and] eloquent," nevertheless condemns Don Juan
as unequivocally as Blagoy praises him:

Don Juan strode to his radiant zenith along a shameful path
(like the Baron and Salieri—after all, they also thought that
they were pursuing lofty goals) . . . violating at every step not
so much divine as human laws, subordinating everything else
to his "I want." The series of "crimes" of Don Juan is crowned

by his invitation to the knight-commander. Regardless of what the commander may have been, Don Juan is gibing at, mocking, degrading a man—albeit a dead man—and insulting his widow. This cannot be forgiven.[6]

Thus Pushkin, in the third of the "little tragedies," has set us a mystery that, over a century and a half later, we still cannot feel we have truly grasped. Nevertheless, critics continue to make the effort. What follows is one possible interpretation of the play, the interpretation I find to be the most consistent with the text and the most compelling.

In turning to the legend of Don Juan as a subject, Pushkin was placing himself in what was already a long literary and dramatic tradition. By the end of the eighteenth century, its founding work—Tirso de Molina's *El burlador de Sevilla y convidado de pietra* (The Mocker of Seville and the Stone Guest)—had inspired two works of genius, Molière's *Le festin de pierre* (The Stone Guest) and Mozart's *Don Giovanni*, as well as a host of lesser imitators. One of them, a pre-Molière *Le festin de pierre* by Villiers, was apparently known to Pushkin, either directly or through a Russian or Polish translation.[7] Among Pushkin's contemporaries, Byron had taken up the subject of Don Juan, although the spectacular plot twists and Europe-wide scope of his narrative poem suggests far less the traditional story of profligacy and retribution than a re-imagining of how Voltaire's Candide might have fared had he possessed extraordinary sex appeal. Closer to the traditional form of the legend, Hoffmann wrote a meditation on Mozart's *Don Giovanni* in the form of a short story in which it is supernaturally revealed to the narrator that it was Doña Anna's true destiny, tragically thwarted, to be the final and redemptive love of Don Giovanni—an interpretation that, it has been suggested, may have affected Pushkin's concept of Doña Anna.

Pushkin retains the basic plot of the legend: the role of Don Juan as a notoriously successful seducer and the horror of all right-minded citizens, his defiant invitation to the statue of the knight-commander whom he has killed in a duel, the statue's appearance in response, and their joint descent into the other world. But within this framework Pushkin creates a unique Don Juan. For Molière and Mozart, Don Juan is a deliberate, aggressive challenger of the laws of God and man. Pushkin's Don Juan doesn't actively defy the law: he simply acts as if it will go away if he doesn't notice it.

As the play begins, we see Don Juan returning from exile (in a nod to Byron, seemingly from England) — and why is he returning? Because he was bored there, and, in particular, because the local women were boring. That, for him, is reason enough to shrug off a royal command and risk the consequences. Or, rather, he cannot even imagine that there will be consequences: after all, nobody will recognize him; or, if somebody does recognize him, he surely won't have the bad luck to run into the king himself; or, if the king does hear about his return, surely the worst that will happen to him is that he'll be exiled again — so what? Just as one is about to dismiss this Don Juan as a thoroughgoing lightweight, suddenly we see an entirely different side of him. He remembers when he was in this same place before, with a past love:

Don Juan: (*Pensively*)

                   Poor Inez!
           She's gone now! how I loved her!

Leporello: Inez! — the black-eyed one. . . . Now I remember,
           For three months you were paying court
           To her; it was all the devil could do to help.

Don Juan: July it was . . . at night. I found strange pleasure
           In gazing at her sorrowful eyes
           And death-pale lips. It's strange,
           You apparently didn't think she was
           A beauty. And in fact, there wasn't
           Much beautiful about her. Her eyes,
           Just her eyes. And her glance . . . I've never seen
           Another glance like that. And her voice

> Was quiet, feeble—like a sick woman's—
> Her husband was a worthless wretch, and stern—
> I found that out too late—Poor Inez! . . .

So Don Juan, who is so heedless of a consequence tomorrow if it interferes with his pleasure today, is after all capable, when a woman does not immediately accept his suit, of courting her assiduously for three months. And Inez, this heroine out of Edgar Allan Poe, with her pallor and her haunting black eyes, with her delicacy, so suggestive of early doom, and the final hint that she met a tragic end—is this a woman whom one would have thought would attract Don Juan, who had just been singing the praises of the fiery, earthy, vital women of Andalusia? Such an attraction suggests a depth in Don Juan that he himself does not understand: he can only repeat: "I found strange pleasure. . . . It's strange."

But if this passage points to the possibility of genuine emotional depth in Don Juan, it also indicates a disturbing irresponsibility about the consequences of his passions. His last two lines suggest that the jealousy of her "stern" husband (Don Juan later uses exactly the same epithet for the notoriously jealous knight-commander) made her life miserable or even caused or hastened her death. Surely, during the three months before Inez surrendered to him, Don Juan could have taken a moment to think about what might happen to her if it became known or suspected that she had committed adultery. Instead, he simply takes the position that he could not have been expected to foresee the consequences: "I found that out too late . . ." Nevertheless, the memory of Inez is a reproach to both master and servant, and both are all too willing to push it away quickly:

Leporello: Well, so, after her came others.
Don Juan: True.
Leporello: And while we're still alive, there'll be still more.

Don Juan: Also true.
Leporello: So what woman in Madrid
              Are we going to go after?
Don Juan: Oh, Laura!
              I'll head straight for her house.
Leporello: That's it.
Don Juan: I'll walk right through her door — and if there's company,
              I'll invite him to make his exit through the window.
Leporello: Of course. And now we've cheered right up.
              Dead women don't trouble us for long.

At this moment Don Juan and Leporello are interrupted by the entrance of a monk. Through this interlocutor we learn Pushkin's version of Don Juan's past, which differs significantly from Molière's and Mozart's treatment of the role of Doña Anna. Here she is not the daughter of the slain knight-commander, but his young widow; and whatever was the cause of the fatal duel between Don Juan and the knight-commander, it was not in defense of Doña Anna's honor, because Don Juan has never seen her. In this dialogue, we again see Don Juan's utter absorption with life in the present: told that the dead man's widow comes every day to weep at his tomb, Don Juan replies, "What strange kind of widow's this? /And not bad-looking?" In Don Juan's view, it is inconceivable that a woman could continue to mourn so long over a man who is gone — unless, of course, she is so lamentably unattractive that she could not hope to find a new lover. The monk's refutation of this possibility is one of Pushkin's little masterpieces of characterization:

> We anchorites must not
> Be tempted by the loveliness of women,
> But lying is a sin: a saint himself could not
> Look unmoved upon her wondrous beauty.

One can just see the good father, having delivered this sentiment with eyes piously rolled heavenward and just the right amount of unctuousness, pausing to engage for a moment in a less-than-holy thought about Doña Anna, rather like Friar Tuck devoutly crossing himself before taking a good chomp out of his capon.

Such praises, followed by a brief, tantalizing glimpse of a heavily veiled Doña Anna, lead Don Juan to an impulsive decision: "Listen, Leporello, / I'm going to meet her." Leporello is appalled at the very thought:

> That's just what we need!
> What next! He's bumped off the husband
> And now he wants to see the widow's tears!
> Shameless!

But Leporello reads altogether too much deliberate malice into the actions of his master. For Don Juan, the matter is simple: Doña Anna is beautiful; she is mysterious; what is more natural than that he should wish to meet her? The fact that he happens to be the man who killed her husband is simply irrelevant to him — so why should it mean anything to her? However, no sooner has Don Juan made this decision than he apparently drops it in favor of one which can be more immediately carried out: the moment has come, after sunset and before moonrise, when he enter the city in the relative safety of darkness, and he seizes his chance.

The scene then shifts to Laura's residence. In contrast to Doña Anna, whose marriage was arranged by her mother and who spent her married life "always kept locked up inside," Laura is a free woman: free to live in her own lodgings, free to earn her own living as an actress, free to choose from among her male admirers the one, or ones, who will receive her favors, for as long or as short a time as she pleases. Freedom, spontaneity, is also the credo of her artistic life; when praised by her guests for a brilliant performance, she replies:

> Yes, today every word,
> Every gesture came out well for me.
> I gave myself up freely to inspiration,
> The words poured out as if they were brought forth,
> Not by slavish memory, but by the heart . . .

Laura insists upon her complete freedom of action to such a degree that she simply takes no responsibility for how her words or deeds affect others. When one of her guests becomes angry at her for expressing her admiration for Don Juan, the man who killed his brother, she replies: "Is it my fault, that constantly / That name keeps coming to my tongue?" as if she could not control what she said — unlikely for a professional actress.

Along with unlimited freedom and spontaneity, Laura values intensity: overlooking all the admirers who have done nothing but pay her conventional compliments, she chooses as her favorite the only one who has dared to rebuke and even insult her. For her, his anger is the proof of a passionate nature, and thus attractive:

> You, madman! You stay here with me,
> You've caught my fancy; you reminded me
> Of Don Juan, the way you scolded me
> And clenched your teeth and gnashed them.

This is the second time that Laura has invoked Don Juan; previously she had sung a song for which he had written the lyrics. Her relationship to her "faithful friend and fickle lover" is based not solely on sexual attraction (although that certainly exists), but on a recognition of the similarity of their values. For what makes Don Juan heroic — or, if one prefers, antiheroic — is precisely the strength of his passions and his courageous refusal to accept any limitation on his freedom and spontaneity. To achieve his desire he is willing to risk any consequence, whether it be death in a duel or condemnation by law and public opinion. He is not only a grandee by blood, someone whose face would be known to the king himself; he is also a grandee in spirit, a figure so compelling and memorable that the very idea that he could disguise himself strikes Leporello as ludicrous.

But such power, which is admirable when it is accompanied by a sense of moral responsibility, readily becomes destructive when it is not—a point already suggested by Don Juan's recollection of Inez's tragic fate. We are again reminded of his destructive side, as a man who has killed another and acknowledges no guilt over it, in the scene with Laura, when her admirer Don Carlos is identified as the brother of a man killed by Don Juan in a duel. Whether or not Carlos is the brother of the knight-commander (the point is unclear), certainly the "gloomy guest" in this scene plays a role reminiscent of the "stone guest" of the legend, by warning this female Don Juan of the consequences if she does not repent. The law of moral consequences that Don Carlos invokes, however, is not that of medieval Catholicism, with its threat of supernatural intervention or the flames of hell, but that of the ancient Greeks, that character is fate and that one enjoys or endures the results of what one has chosen to become:

> You're young now . . . and you'll still be young
> For five or six more years. You'll draw
> The men around you six more years,
> To pay you court and give you presents,
> To sing you serenades at night,
> And for your sake to kill each other
> In darkness at the crossroads. But when
> The time comes that your eyes have sunk,
> Their lids grown wrinkled and discolored,
> And your hair is streaked with gray,
> And men start calling you "old woman,"
> Then—what will you say?

From these words, one can picture Laura's fate as being very much like that of the elderly Countess in "The Queen of Spades." The Countess, too, was a great beauty in her youth, "la Vénus moscovite" whose demands and caprices were indulged by her many admirers; but when time had diminished her beauty and habit intensified her utter self-centeredness, she predictably ends up all but forgotten by the very beau monde that had once celebrated her.

Just as Don Juan refuses to consider the possible unwelcome consequences of his unlawful return to Madrid, or of his courtship of Inez, so Laura refuses to consider the all-too-likely future that Don Carlos points out to her:

> Then? Why should
> I think of that? What talk is this?
> Or do you always have such thoughts?
> Come to the balcony. How calm the sky is,
> The air is warm and still, the night is fragrant
> With scents of lime and laurel, the moon
> Shines radiant in the deep dark blue,
> And the watchman cries, "A-a-all's well!" . . .
> And far off, to the north—in Paris—
> Perhaps the sky is gray with clouds,
> Cold rain is falling, the wind howls.
> But what is that to us? Look, Carlos,
> I'm ordering you to smile . . .
> There you go!

Unquestionably Laura's response is beautiful as poetry; but it is also an evasion. The beauty of her words is not surprising; according to Doña Anna, public opinion also describes Don Juan as "eloquent." The danger is that he uses his eloquence in the cause of seduction. And what Laura is doing is also unquestionably seduction—leading Don Carlos away from what he himself knows to be right, as indicated by his response of combined condemnation and attraction: "Sweet demon!"

And thus Don Carlos, the spokesman for the law of moral consequences, himself becomes an example of it. He is aware of the "demonic," destructive nature of Laura's attractiveness; yet he chooses to stay with her. The results of so choosing against his own better judgment become immediately obvious with the entrance of Don Juan. In one sense, from Don Carlos's point of view, it hardly matters that the man who enters to stake his own competing claim on Laura's favor is Don Juan. Any man who made such an entrance, at such a time, would inevitably provoke a duel; duelling, as Don Carlos has already pointed out, is part of the potential cost of being one of Laura's admirers. The only real difference made by the fact that the rival is Don Juan rather than someone else is that while Don Juan is ready to offer the usual courtesies of the duelling code regarding time and place ("Tomorrow I'll be at your service"), Don Carlos's hatred of this man leads him to make the socially inappropriate demand of a fight on the spot, in Laura's room. This demand reveals the the ultimately shallow and selfish nature of Don Carlos's attraction to Laura: not only does he not try to spare her the sight of possible bloodshed, but he disregards the danger of legal consequences to her if someone is injured or killed in her apartment. His lack of any real concern for Laura, however, is more than matched by her lack of any real concern, not only for him, but even for his successful rival. Laura's first response to Don Juan's announcement of his victory — "Get up, Laura, it's all over" — is not relief that the Don Juan (whose praises she was just proclaiming only a few minutes before) is still alive, but anger at the mess he's gotten her into:

> What's this?
> Killed? That's great! And in my room!
> So what do I do now, you shameless devil?
> How do I get rid of him?

Don Juan again shows his irresponsibility by responding with the suggestion that maybe Don Carlos isn't dead after all—a suggestion so self-evidently contrary to the facts that it only encourages Laura's anger. Forced to admit that he has killed his rival, Don Juan simply shrugs: "What could I do? He asked for it." For Laura, who is equally irresponsible, such an answer is more endearing than exasperating, and her anger drops to a grumble, a reproach more appropriate to someone who had played a bad practical joke than someone who has just killed a man:

> Eh, Don Juan,
> What a nuisance. Up to your old tricks,
> But never guilty . . .

Yet Don Juan's claim of "not guilty" is immediately undercut by the interchange between himself and Laura which follows, as he tells her what we already know: that he came to Madrid deliberately, despite his knowledge that the relatives of his previous victim would still want revenge against him, and that he specifically came to seek out Laura, despite his knowledge that she was not the type of woman to pine away for an absent lover. Granted, he did not know what the specific result of his actions would be; but he nevertheless chose a line of conduct that necessarily involved the risk of a violent confrontation.

Don Carlos's fate thus is the result of the characters and choices of all three persons involved in the scene—an event that, if not inevitable, was certainly foreseeable. More than that, it is a foreshadowing of Don Juan's own fate. Each man is attracted to a woman whom his better judgment (had he listened to it) would have tell him to stay away from, and at the moment when each one has just begun to enjoy her favor, he is destroyed by a figure out of the woman's past who reemerges as a romantic rival. Don Juan, indeed, speaks to Laura as if he had a claim upon her fidelity: "How many times have you cheated on me / While I was gone?" She, of course, refuses to yield her freedom, retorting,

"What about you, skirt-chaser?" But her very response reaffirms the bond between then: she is his because she is like him. Don Juan agrees to put off the discussion of their past actions until "later," a "later" that, one can be sure, will never come unless it is convenient to both of them. For the moment, all that they want is to give themselves up to their passion—a passion that apparently is not even disturbed by the presence of Don Carlos's body, which Don Juan does not plan to remove until he himself has to leave, just before it gets light.

But even Don Juan, for all his recklessness, realizes that after this additional killing he can no longer follow his original plan of entering Madrid as if nothing were wrong. This, however, is no more allowed to stand in the way of his previously aroused interest in Doña Anna than is the minor detail (from his point of view) that he is her husband's killer. Instead, he simultaneously evades the law and promotes his courtship by disguising himself as a monk in the monastery where the knight-commander is buried. He is oblivious to both the ludicrous side of the situation (Don Juan as a monk!) and the blasphemous one (a layman representing himself as if he were in holy orders and trying to seduce a woman in a Catholic cemetery, i.e., on consecrated ground). All that concerns him is whether his stratagem will work. And although it has started off promisingly—"every day / I see my charming widow, and she, / It seems to me, has noticed"—one aspect of this budding relationship disturbs him:

> She should already be here. Without her,
> I think, the knight-commander must be bored.
> What a giant he's been made into here!
> What shoulders! What a Hercules!
> The man himself was small and puny,
> If he were here and stood on tiptoe,
> His fingertip couldn't reach to his own nose.
> When we went out beyond the Escurial,

He stuck himself upon my sword and died
Like a dragonfly upon a pin—but still
He was proud and bold, and stern of spirit . . .

This is a new tone in Don Juan's voice: he speaks of the knight-commander, not with the courtesy it befits a grandee to show to an enemy of equal rank, but mockingly, sneeringly, even vulgarly. Clearly, something has stung Don Juan; the thought of the knight-commander in some way uncontrollably rankles him. He reveals why in the words, "Without her, / I think, the knight-commander must be bored." Don Juan regards the statue as if it were the knight-commander himself, a still-living claimant of Doña Anna's affection. The fact that the statue is oversized fittingly expresses the way in which Doña Anna's husband has come to occupy a larger place in Don Juan's consciousness in death than he ever did while alive. Don Juan tries to diminish his rival (literally and figuratively) by mockery, but so far from succeeding in doing so, his disrespect strikes even him as excessive—a sense which forces him to make unwilling amends in the grudging tribute of the final line.

Significantly, this is the first time Don Juan has expressed jealousy of a rival. He has no apparent concern about Laura's other lovers, provided that they are willing to "make their exit through the window" as soon as he arrives. The thought of Inez's husband rouses him to indignation, but not to jealousy. By contrast, although he has not yet spoken a single word to Doña Anna, he already regards himself as having a claim on her exclusive faithfulness, to the point that he is jealous even of her attention to her husband's grave. Such an unprecedented feeling on Don Juan's part gives substance to his later claim to Doña Anna that his love for her is different from his feelings for all the other women he has known. Despite all the evidence of his own past to the contrary, no doubt Don Juan believes it when he tells Doña Anna that he is prepared now to be exclusively faithful to one woman: "command, and then I'll breathe / For only you."

This same motif of love for Doña Anna combined with jealousy toward her past spontaneously reemerges in Don Juan's improvised response to Doña Anna's invitation to him to pray with her:

I only watch you from afar with reverence,
And when your head is quietly bowed down,
Black tresses spilling on the marble's whiteness —
Then it seems to me an angel comes
To honor this grave with a secret visit,
And in my troubled heart I cannot find
The words to pray. I marvel then in silence
And think — happy man, whose cold marble
Is warmed by her celestial breathing
And sprinkled with her tears of love.

Paradoxically, it is precisely this jealousy that helps Don Juan to approach Doña Anna. For Doña Anna, too, is still extremely conscious of the hold of the past upon the present, of what she sees as her husband's claim upon her faithfulness even after his death. She is, it would seem, not a completely inconsolable widow: she is not above noticing that the same young and handsome monk has been in the cemetery every day. Indeed, she is so interested in speaking to him that she starts with a decidedly clumsy opening line, asking forgiveness for disturbing him in his (presumed) meditations — and thereby, of course, disturbing him all the more. Nevertheless, she strives to preserve the image that she presents to herself and to the world of an unwaveringly faithful widow. She can engage a handsome monk in conversation and at the same time regard herself as faithful to her husband, because she is merely asking the monk to join her in prayers for her husband's soul. And her reaction when Don Juan confesses that he is not a monk, and that he is in love with her, shows far less indignation either at the fact that a suitor dared to approach her at all while she was in mourning, or that he resorted to a deception to do it, than fear of scandal: "And here, right by the grave! . . . If someone came in!" Don Juan's jealousy of the knight-commander reassures her that she indeed is faithful and is perceived as such. And Don Juan, urged on by his genuine consciousness of rivalry with the dead man, is inspired to the verbal extravagance of a poet-improviser upon the theme that she has set: to profess to regard her as unapproachably faithful to her late husband while at the same time paying a determined courtship to her. Thus he declares himself "an unlucky man, victim of a hopeless passion," in contrast to that "happy man" at whose tomb she weeps; he speaks of death and burial as the only way of obtaining any favor from her, even so little as the touch of her foot upon his grave, in contrast to the attention that she lavishes upon the knight-commander's tomb; he asserts that only if he were mad would he have any hope that his love would touch her heart.

Such declarations are something that a devout and dutiful young woman like Doña Anna has never been taught about and does not know how to respond to. Clearly, a woman who asks a question like, "And have you loved me a long time?" is not unwilling to hear a profession of love; but upon receiving an appropriately impassioned response, she is frightened. Without breaking off this suddenly established relationship, she tries to exert some control over it:

> Leave—this is not the place
> For such words and such madness. Tomorrow
> Come to my house. If you will swear
> To show the same respect to me as now,
> I'll receive you; but after night falls, late—
> I haven't seen anyone since the day
> That I was widowed . . .

One cannot help but be struck by Doña Anna's action: in a culture where any respectable woman would be carefully chaperoned, she invites a man whom she barely knows to her house alone, late at night, confident that despite the compromising nature of the situation and

the obvious temptation it provides, he will show her "respect" and regard her as inviolable. Unless one assumes, as Leporello does, that she's
a complete hypocrite ("Oh widows, you're all the same"), the only
possible explanations for such astonishing conduct seem to be either
that she is so utterly naive, so unfamiliar with the power of sexual passion, that she doesn't realize what she may be getting into, or that she
is simply too weak a character, too easily dominated, to be able to decisively refuse a man as determined as Don Juan. True, no sooner does
she make this promise than she becomes frightened by the position her
unasked-for suitor has put her in, and tries to get rid of him by waving
her piety in his face; but at the same time, she doesn't want to retract
her offer:

Doña Anna: Now leave me.
Don Juan: One minute longer.
Doña Anna: No, then clearly I must go. . . . Besides, my prayers
Have completely slipped my mind. You distracted me
With worldly speeches, to which my ears
Have long been unaccustomed. — Tomorrow
I will receive you.

Small wonder that such a man of the world as Don Juan, either not
understanding or brushing aside Doña Anna's scruples, receives her
offer in a rather different spirit than she would regard it as having been
made, and boasts to Leporello of having obtained a "rendezvous."

   In reply, Leporello — evidently as convinced of the knight-commander's "presence" in the form of his statue as his master is — replies,
"And the knight-commander? What'll he have to say?" Don Juan re-
assumes his earlier tone of scoffing at his rival:

What do you think — he's going to be jealous?
Not likely; he's a reasonable man
And probably has cooled off some after dying

These words have a particularly jarring ring coming from the man responsible for that death. But the man whom Don Juan himself had to acknowledge as "proud and bold, and stern of spirit" cannot be dismissed so easily. Leporello persists in his fear of the knight-commander, insisting that the statue looks angry. At this point, when Don Juan is passionately excited at the thought that Doña Anna is almost his, he feels that he has been reminded quite enough of the obstacle that the thought of her dead husband presents. With characteristic impulsiveness and audacity, Don Juan decides to break the hold that in spite of himself the statue has gained over his imagination, by yielding to that hold and thereby, as he anticipates, demonstrating its meaninglessness. He will treat the statue as if it truly were a living being, his rival, and issue it a challenge: to stop him from claiming Doña Anna as his own. And when, as he expects, the statue fails to do any such thing, he will have demonstrated to himself once and for all that it is merely a lifeless, powerless object, that the spirit of the knight-commander cannot stand in the way of his future happiness.

Leporello, who has no more courage than one would expect from someone holding the traditionally unheroic position of valet, takes this challenge at face value: suppose the statue really does come? An infuriated husband is, no doubt, something Leporello has seen Don Juan deal with before, but what defense is there against the spirit of a dead man, inhabiting a body made not of flesh and blood, but of stone? In an attempt to protect himself against whatever retribution the statue may exact, Leporello carefully addresses it in as courteous a manner as possible, thus making a wonderfully inappropriate contrast with the studiedly insulting message he has been ordered to convey:

Most glorious and handsome statue!
My lord Don Juan respectfully requests
The pleaure of your company. . . . My God, I can't,
I'm too afraid.

Only the fact that the servant is more afraid of the real and tangible threats made by his master than of a vague and potential supernatural danger induces him to convey the invitation to the statue at all; and when it confirms his dread by making an actual response — nodding its head — he collapses in shrieks of terror.

If, even before Leporello's outcry, Don Juan was already angered by the seemingly inexplicable power of this dead man who somehow could not be forgotten, Leporello's terrified acknowledgment of that power drives Don Juan to an extreme of determined fury. Brushing his servant aside, Don Juan steps up to the statue and issues his challenge, not in the grandee-to-grandee tone he used with Don Carlos ("Tomorrow I'll be at your service"), but with the sneer of a teenage boy making a dare:

> I request, knight-commander, that you pay
> A visit to your widow, where I'll be tomorrow,
> And stand guard at the door. Well? Are you coming?

The statue's nod in response staggers Don Juan for a moment, and he cries, "Oh God!" But then he regains his self-possession sufficiently to resume his usual method of dealing with unwelcome occurrences — by ignoring them. He tells Leporello simply, "Let's go," and once they no longer have the reminder of the statue's presence in front of them, not a word will be spoken about the extraordinary sign they have both witnessed.

How is it possible that a man who had received such a warning would go through with his plan to win Doña Anna? In this lies the essence of the "little tragedies": each one is an examination of the type of single-minded, self-willed passion that blinds a person, so that the warnings of reason and conscience are equally powerless, and the path of self-destruction is deliberately chosen. Don Juan's passion for Doña Anna, his determination to make her his own, is so great that no threat, not even a supernatural one, will keep him from the rendezvous.

Initially, Don Juan and Doña Anna take up positions unchanged from the day before: Doña Anna is clearly pleased to listen to the adoring speeches of "Don Diego," but still determinedly maintains her faithfulness to her dead husband; Don Juan is still left to the unsatisfactory role of rival with "that happy departed one" who won what her new suitor can only dream of. When Doña Anna explains that her marriage to the wealthy Don Alvaro was arranged by her mother, Don Juan replies:

> Happy man! he laid his empty treasures
> At the feet of a goddess, and for that
> He tasted heavenly bliss! Oh, if only
> I'd known you then, how rapturously
> My rank, my wealth, everything I had,
> I'd have given for one favorable glance.
> I would have been a slave to your sacred will,
> Your every whim I would have closely studied,
> To fulfill it in advance; so that your life
> Would have been enchantment never-ending.
> Alas! — Fate decreed otherwise for me.

One can imagine the appeal such words would have to a woman like Doña Anna, whose whole life has been arranged, first by her mother and then by her husband, and who has never been in a situation where her own will was paramount. His suggestion that a new world of sexual and personal freedom could be open to her is deeply enticing and at the same time profoundly contrary to her strong sense of propriety. Her reply, although nominally addressed to "Don Diego," is in fact an exhortation to herself, an attempt to overcome the temptation posed by her suitor, not only by invoking her duty, but also by arguing to herself that no new lover could offer her more than her devoted husband had:

Diego, stop it; when I listen to you,
I commit a sin—I mustn't love you,
A widow must be faithful to the grave.
If only you knew how much Don Alvaro
Loved me! Oh, surely Don Alvaro
Wouldn't have received an enamoured lady
If he'd been widowed.—He'd have been faithful
To spousal love.

Again and again Don Juan comes up against the same wall: Doña Anna is attracted to him, she has all but fallen in love with him—and yet always his dead rival, the knight-commander, stands in the way.

In response, Don Juan boldly decides to go for all or nothing, to force Doña Anna to choose between them. So far, Don Juan's incognito as "Diego" has allowed Doña Anna to finesse the issue of which man, her dead husband or her new would-be lover, has her ultimate loyalty. But if she knows that her suitor is also her husband's killer, then inevitably she must decide where her loyalty lies. Such a revelation, of course, cannot simply be blurted out. Instead, Don Juan makes his first move with a carefully calculated "slip," by adding to his recurring statements of jealousy a new theme, that of guilt:

Do not torment my heart,
Doña Anna, by this eternal mentioning
Of your husband. You've punished me enough,
Though perhaps the punishment's deserved.

The first thing that Doña Anna fears in response to this vague admission of guilt—a reflection, no doubt, of her own uneasy conscience— is that "Diego" is being unfaithful:

There are no holy bonds uniting you
To any other—isn't that so? When you love me,
You do no wrong to me or in Heaven's eyes.

Don Juan's reply—"To you! God!"—implicitly declares that his guilt
is not that of adultery (a "wrong ... in Heaven's eyes"). Yet by refusing
to confide in Doña Anna, by suggesting that there is some circumstance that could part them, Don Juan arouses Doña Anna's fear of
losing this new admirer. She thus tries to hold on to him by committing
herself to him more deeply: she promises "Diego" that, if he will tell
her the truth, she will forgive him anything in advance. However, she
makes this promise thoughtlessly, supposing that in fact there is little
to forgive:

And how could you have injured me?
I didn't know you—I have no enemies
And never had any. My husband's killer
Is the only one.

Don Juan, thoroughly in command of the whole conversation and recognizing this as the crucial moment, takes advantage of his incognito
to probe Doña Anna's feelings towards her husband's killer:

Don Juan: In your heart
      Do you nurse hate for him?
Doña Anna: As honor demands.
      But you're trying to distract me
      From my question, Don Diego—
      I order ...
Don Juan: What if you should chance
      To meet Don Juan?
Doña Anna: I'd plunge my dagger
      Into the villain's heart.

Such purely abstract hate for a man whom Doña Anna has never met, motivated simply by social convention (what "honor demands"), is clearly no more than a rhetorical threat, and Don Juan unhesitatingly calls Doña Anna's bluff: "Doña Anna, / Where's your dagger? Here's my breast."

Doña Anna is stunned by this admission, paralyzed by the suddenness with which she is placed between unwelcome alternatives: either to reject the suitor who has already gained so powerful a hold on her feelings, or to condone the death of her husband. And Don Juan, playing winner takes all, forces the choice on her as bluntly as possible, by denying any mitigating circumstances for his actions:

> I killed
> Your husband; and I don't regret it —
> And there's no repentance in me.

Only when Doña Anna faints does Don Juan realize that he has pushed her too hard, and tries to resume his earlier persona: "your Diego / Your slave is at your feet." Reversing his defiance of moral censure, his absence of repentance, he now presents himself as a man newly conscious of the evil he has done and ready to reform:

> No doubt you've heard him spoken of
> As a criminal, a monster. Doña Anna,
> The stories, it may be, are partly true,
> My weary conscience, may be, bears the burden
> Of a heavy load of evil. Indeed, I have
> Long followed willingly the path of vice,
> But since the moment when I first saw you,
> It seems to me that I have been reborn.
> In loving you, I've come to love the good,
> And humbly, for the first time in my life,
> I bend my trembling knees before it.

At this point Doña Anna makes the mistake (to be followed by generations of literary critics) of allowing Don Juan's words to serve as the springboard for an argument over whether his claim to be converted to virtue, "reborn," is genuine or merely a seducer's ploy, and whether his love for Doña Anna means more to him than any of his other romances. Such a discussion, however, obscures the fundamental issue. For all his professed devotion to virtue, Don Juan still fails to acknowledge one of the most basic laws of the moral universe: that life is not a bankruptcy court in which one can have all one's debts forgiven and start again with a clean slate; that no matter how sincerely one repents of one's wrongdoing, the consequences of that wrongdoing nevertheless must be borne. It is this realization whih underlies "Remembrance" ("Воспоминание"), a poem written by Pushkin two years before the "little tragedies," which ends with the lines:

> Relentless Memory will wordlessly unwind
>   Her long, long scroll for my inspection;
> With loathing I peruse the record of my years,
>   I execrate, I quail and falter,
> I utter bitter plaints, and hotly flow my tears,
>   But those sad lines I cannot alter.[8]

It would be possible for Don Juan to repent the knight-commander's death (although, by his own admission, he does not), and for Doña Anna to forgive him. But the death itself is an unchangeable fact; and no matter how sincerely or "virtuously" Don Juan may love Doña Anna or Doña Anna may love him, there is a morally impassible barrier between a killer and the widow of his victim.

For a moment, Doña Anna realizes this, as she tells Don Juan, "Ah, if only I could hate you! / But all the same we have to part." But no sooner does she say this than, like Don Carlos, despite her own knowledge of the danger and dishonor of her actions, she allows herself to surrender to the lure of the "sweet demon." She offers no resistance to

Don Juan's straightforward demand (it can hardly be called a request) for another rendezvous the following night, beyond murmuring, "Oh Don Juan, how weak of heart I am." Don Juan, taking advantage of her willingness to yield, pushes ahead, asking for a kiss to "seal your pardon." Doña Anna, well aware that it is not exactly Christian forgiveness that he is seeking, still does not refuse him, but only tries to evade his request — "It's time now, go." In response, Don Juan tries to present what he is asking for, not as the momentous decision of rejecting her dead husband in favor of the man who killed him, but as something so trivial that it would hardly be worth mentioning: "A single kiss, cold, peaceful . . ." And Doña Anna once again gives in — indeed, she now picks up Don Juan's trick of laying the blame for her own choices on others, speaking as if he had somehow forced her to give him a kiss: "How importunate you are! Well, there it is."

At this moment, it appears, Don Juan is triumphant. The moral law that actions have consequences, it seems, has been overcome through his determination to "forget" the past, and his ability to persuade Doña Anna to do likewise. And then, at the very instant of Don Juan's triumph, the banished past reasserts its power: the statue of the knight-commander enters.

This is the crucial moment of the play, as indicated by its very title, which is not *Don Juan*, but *The Stone Guest*. From the moment of its entrance, the statue is a completely dominating presence, incapable of being resisted and indifferent to any response Don Juan may offer. Don Juan's concern for the fallen Doña Anna is dismissed with the abrupt command, "Leave her" (the Russian is just as terse and jarring: "Брось ее"). Don Juan, to his credit, initially responds courageously to the statue's appearance, freely obeying its command, "Give me your hand," but his bravery has no effect on the course of action. When his courage fails and he tries to withdraw his hand, crying, "Leave me alone, let go — let go of me," his words are ignored. In contrast to Mozart's Commendatore, whose final unheeded demand for Don Juan's repentance clearly reflects a Christian outlook, the speech and actions of Pushkin's knight-commander suggest the impassiveness and inexorability of an agent of Fate.

The fate which the statue represents, however, is not a random one, but the very fate which Don Juan himself invited: "You bade me, I have come." As the miserly knight is destroyed by the simultaneous demands of two incompatible desires — his all-consuming passion for gold and his wish to be respected as a knight — so, too, Don Juan becomes the victim of his own impossible demands. Unwaveringly, from the play's beginning until its end, Don Juan claims the right to forget the past, to ignore unwelcome circumstances, to be exempt from the consequences of his actions. At the same time, once he has fallen in love with Doña Anna, he lays claim to her exclusive fidelity, and professes the same fidelity in return. But fidelity means that a choice, once made, will be adhered to, whatever its consequences. Indeed, Doña Anna asserts that fidelity should be unaffected even by death: "A widow should be faithful to the grave." This extreme view contains a kernel of truth: a remarried widow (or widower) who does not preserve the memory of the former spouse, but rather tries to deny or obliterate it, is in effect committing an act of posthumous betrayal. It is precisely such a betrayal into which Don Juan wishes to lure Doña Anna, for only by denying her husband's memory could she accept his killer as her lover. Don Juan still refuses to accept responsibility for his own past action by acknowledging that he can have no rightful claim upon Doña Anna; but he does feel guilt and unease about the insult that his planned seduction will inflict upon the memory of the knight-commander. His invitation to the statue is thus an act of bravado, an attempt to silence his own qualms. But instead of escaping his guilt, he is destroyed by it. For, as students of history and psychology both know, when a denied and buried past is again acknowledged and summoned, it may well turn out, like the dead knight-commander, to possess a power greater than that of the living.

Survival and Memory:
A Feast During the Plague

ONE IS TEMPTED to say that *A Feast During the Plague* could be more descriptively entitled *A Debate During the Plague*. Its characters do not simply give themselves up to revelry as a means of forgetting about their own danger, like the storytellers of Boccaccio's *Decameron*. Rather, their thoughts constantly return to a single question: what is the response of an individual to a catastrophe that has enveloped the community as a whole but he or she personally has so far escaped? Is it possible to save oneself by turning one's back on the doomed community, or does one's own humanity demand solidarity with other human beings even in their agony? And what bond—if any—remains between the saved and the lost, the living and the dead? The very image of a feast during the Plague poses this question: for a feast, a communal meal, reflects the human need for society; and yet this small society that is feasting is acting as if the sufferings of the larger society around it do not exist. This contrast between the solidarity of the revelers in their small group — organized, like a society, with a recognized authority — and their indifference to the larger society is underscored by the very first words of *Feast:*

> Mr. Chairman! I call to mind
> Someone whom we all know well,
> A man whose jokes and funny stories,
> Witty retorts and observations,
> So biting in their mock pomposity,
> Have enlivened our table talk
> And driven away the gloom which now
> The plague, our guest, is shedding
> Over the most brilliant minds.

From this speech alone one can form a mental picture of the speaker, who significantly is not given a name, but is known only as "the young man": a man for whom a "feast" means not just eating and drinking, but most of all companionship, intellectual gaiety, a sense of freedom — in short, a young man not so different from Pushkin and his friends in their first youth. Is it so surprising that such a man wants to live, wants to forget about the danger around him? But despite their best efforts, the small society of the revelers in fact cannot isolate itself from the sufferings around it:

> Two days ago our laughter crowned
> His stories; it isn't possible
> That in our merry feasting we should
> Forget Jackson. Here's his chair,

Sitting empty, as if waiting for
A good companion—but he's gone away
To a cold lodging underground . . .

Thus the question the play becomes personalized: what link is there between the safe and the suffering, the quick and the dead, when those who are stricken include not merely fellow citizens or casual acquaintances, but one's own friends and family, those to whom one is closest? Here is where the "young man's" love of life and joy curdles into an ugly egotism. He has no more real concern for his fellow revelers than he has for the larger society. His friends are important to him only insofar as they can distract his attention from the one thing that really frightens him, the possibility of his own death. Despite his praise of Jackson, the "young man" is so little moved by Jackson's death that he can propose to have the feast go on without the slightest acknowledgment that anything is different:

But many of us still live, and we
Have no cause to be grieving. So
I propose we drink a toast to him
With glasses clinking and with shouts
As if he were alive.

By contrast, for the Chairman, the revelers form a genuine society, not merely a random collection of individuals, and the loss of one of them is meaningful to them all:

He was the first
Of our group to go. In silence
We'll drink to honor him.

Such a spirit, of course, if extended beyond "our group" to society as a whole, would result in the breakup of the "feast." To prevent such a breakup, the Chairman has to justify his willingness to pause for such a moment of solemn remembrance in a manner that the "feasters" will accept. Hee does this by asserting that a moment of grief, far from burdening them, will merely enhance their subsequent enjoyment:

Sing, Mary, something sad and haunting,
To make us turn again to our merrymaking
With a wilder spirit . . .

Mary's song again brings to the fore the question of communal catastrophe and individual response. The ballad opens by evoking the now-vanished happiness of a small Scottish village. In this simple but reassuringly familiar place, there is no such thing as an isolated individual. Everything is "we": our church, our children, our fields. And in the disaster of the two following stanzas, everything is still "we." Every form of familiar activity, every pre-Plague institution, has been equally destroyed. The whole community—living and dead alike—has converged on the graveyard; all the living are gathered there to bury and honor their dead; survivors pray not for themselves but for the souls of the dead, and through their prayers are still united with those whom they have lost; the dead even physically become a community, as the filling-up of the graveyard means that each new grave must be dug closer to its neighbors.

Not until after the third of the song's five stanzas does its narrator even emerge as a separate individual, an "I"; and she does so only to realize with calm dignity that there is no reason why she should escape the common fate: "If my springtime too is blighted, / If the grave my lot must be." In her own mind she is already among the dead, already sees her own funeral, and yet she speaks of it without a word of lament or of fear for herself. Yet the level tone of her voice is not that of one numbed by community tragedy or ready to resign from life. She loves life, she wants it passionately—but for her beloved Edmund, not herself. It is he who must actively try to save his life, who must take the precautions that one feels she would not bother to take: he who must stay away when she is stricken, must not approach too closely to her body, must leave the village in search of somewhere safer. Such seeming disrespect to her will in fact be fulfilling her supreme wish: that he live on when she cannot, for his life, his well-being, is more important to her than her own is. Indeed, just as her death agony is merely a part of the agony of her village, so Edmund's life and her life will be indissolubly united:

> When the plague ends — then come visit
> Where my poor dust found its rest,
> And Jenny will be true to Edmund
> E'en in her place among the blest!

As Walsingham points out in his response, this song is itself a testimony to the indissoluble bond between the living and the dead, as folk tradition tenaciously preserves the memory of an agony of which all physical traces have long since vanished. Such an example of solidarity with and faithfulness to the dead can hardly be welcome to the revelers. Thus Walsingham's response tries to refute Mary's song by emphasizing the discontinuity between "earlier days" and the present. He speaks of the difference between the former agony of "then" and the natural beauty and peacefulness of "now" (although there is, of course, no reason to assume that what Pushkin would elsewhere call "indifferent Nature" was any less beautiful in the plague year) and downplays the significance of folk memory as much as possible:

> In earlier days the plague, it's clear,
> Visited your native hills and dales
> And moans of sorrow then were heard
> Along those brooks and streams which now
> Flow so peaceful and so merry
> Through your land's rude paradise.

That gloomy year, in which there fell so many
Among the brave, the beautiful and good,
Has hardly left a trace, except the memory
Of simple shepherds, singing an old song,
A sad and sweet one . . .

Walsingham's mixture of admiration and condescension toward the song is worthy of an aristocrat in a Paris salon in 1770 toying with fashionable Rousseauism: it's very sweet, of course, and unquestionably touching, but sophisticated people like ourselves really can't be expected to regard it as anything more than a brief diversion.

Mary, by contrast, takes the song completely seriously. Just as its lyrics point to a real historical event, so when she sings it, she thinks of her own past; just as it speaks of the constancy of love—the love of man and woman—so she remembers the constancy of the love of her own parents:

Oh, if only I had never sung
To anyone outside my parents' croft!
How they loved to listen to their Mary;
It seems to me that I can hear myself
Singing in the house where I was born.
My voice was sweeter then—it was
The voice of innocence . . .

But, unlike the Jenny of the song, Mary has broken faith with those who loved her. She too is one of the revelers at the table. She can still be moved, even profoundly moved, by the image of faithful, self-abnegating love depicted in the song. But she feels it as an impossible ideal. Between her past and her present self she feels an irremediable gap, an unbridgeable discontinuity: now an urban prostitute, she cannot love as she once could when she was an innocent village girl.

In an effective dramatic contrast, Mary, the prostitute with the heart of gold, is answered by the cynical, jaded prostitute Louisa. Picking up the theme stated by the "young man" — "many of us still live, and we / Have no cause to be grieving" — Louisa takes it for granted that the purpose of life is to enjoy oneself as best one may. No matter what the circumstances may be, the only people who grieve, or even believe in another's grief, are either fools or shamming:

> . . . But there are still
> Some fools who like to melt when women cry,
> Who'll swallow it hook, line, and sinker.
> She's decided that her tearful look
> Can't be resisted — if that's what she thought
> About her laugh, no doubt we'd see her
> Grinning all the time . . .

One might think that Louisa's selfishness would make her emotionally stronger than Mary's hopeless yearning for faithful love. After all, as the anxiety of Jenny for Edmund underscores, to love another means to make oneself vulnerable, to fear for that person — so wouldn't a person who cares about no one except herself be better equipped to face a catastrophe? But the reverse proves to be the case: when the revelers are confronted by a cart of bodies being hauled to a common grave, Louise is overcome by terror and faints. By contrast, Mary — no less threatened with death than Louise — is able to lay aside whatever fear the sight evokes in her in order to comfort the distress of the very woman who only a moment before had sneered at her:

> Sister of my shame and sorrow,
> Lean upon my breast.

In these few words of matchless humility and simplicity, Mary recognizes the bond between Louisa's sufferings and her own. For Louisa, by contrast, what makes the suffering represented by the death cart terrifying is its alienness. She perceives its driver as inhuman, the plague victims as incomprehensible, perhaps unreal:

> I dreamed I saw
> A hideous demon, black all over, with white eyes . . .
> He called me to his wagon. Lying in it
> Were the dead—and they were muttering
> In some hideous, unknown language.
> Tell me: was it after all a dream?
> Did the cart pass?

It is worth noting that in Wilson it is the driver who mutters in an unknown language; in Pushkin it is the dead who do so—a change that, in all likelihood, is the result of a grammatical misunderstanding on Pushkin's part. Nevertheless, this is an inspired misunderstanding: for Louisa to perceive the dead as speaking a language unknown to the living emphasizes her inability, unlike Mary, to see the living and the dead as one community.

At this point, the floor is again taken by the first speaker of the play, the "young man," and there is an apparent repetition of its opening situation. The "young man" calls for merriment, which is to be demonstrated by a specific action (the company drinking noisily, Walsingham singing a drinking song). Walsingham answers with a modified counterproposal (for the company to drink in silence, for Walsingham to sing a hymn to the Plague). The accolades with which Walsingham's proposed hymn is received seem to suggest that the revelers are following the same logic that Walsingham followed in requesting Mary's song: they assume that the contemplation of suffering in an artistic work will, by force of contrast, heighten their enjoyment of their own safety.

This parallelism in the circumstances leading up to each song naturally suggests a comparison between the songs themselves. Such a comparison reveals a number of similarities between the songs; and each of these similarities, in turn, points to an underlying dissimilarity. Both songs (if we accept Walsingham's comments on the genesis of Mary's song as correct) are a direct response to actual experience of the Plague. But Mary's song is a folk song, reflecting a communal memory, whereas Walsingham's song is the work of an individual, generated from the profound effect of a personal crisis: as he notes, it is the first time he has ever written a poem. Both Mary's song and Walsingham's song open with the image of a "we"; but while Mary's "we" is that of a small, tightly knit village, Walsingham's "we" is merely that of a group of drinking companions, not necessarily any more closely bound emotionally than the revelers at Walsingham's own table. In both songs, the "we" of the initial stanzas forms a background against which a central theme is played out. In Mary's song, however, the central theme is also a "we," a smaller, but even more intimate one: the two lovers, Edmund and Jenny. By contrast, in Walsingham's song, this central section becomes completely abstract and philosophical:

> There's rapture in the bullets' flight
> And on the mountain's treacherous height,
> And on a ship's deck far from land
> When skies grow dark and waves swell high,
> And in Sahara's blowing sand,
> And when the pestilence is nigh.
>
> All, all that threatens to destroy
> Fills mortal hearts with secret joy
> Beyond our power to explain —
> Perhaps it bodes eternal life!
> And blest is he who can attain
> That ecstasy in storm and strife!

These stanzas show the superiority of Walsingham to his fellow revelers, the superiority which they themselves acknowledge in making him their chairman. They are afraid of death; he is not. Indeed, to him the nearness of death is an experience that sharpens the edge of life, which intensifies one's joy in living. This can be an admirable trait — in the right circumstances. But critics who admire it in Walsingham overlook the price he has paid to achieve it. Human beings are capable of finding a kind of joy in situations of great danger — but only when the danger is to themselves. No one has ever found joy in the knowledge that someone beloved is in danger. Hector does not feel dread before the battle, but Andromache does.

This concern for another, which is the very heart of Mary's song, is completely missing from Walsingham's. In its place is a titanic isolation of spirit, a pride in one's own strength and a delight in matching that strength against the greatest opponents, against the elements, against death itself. It is a song such as Raskolnikov might have written if he had been, not a student in St. Petersburg, but a Cossack on horseback or the captain of a sailing ship. One recalls Raskolnikov's self-mocking description of his logic as "aesthetically flawed" when he realizes that no one except himself would equate the battle of Toulon and the murder of an old woman. Walsingham's logic is also "aesthetically flawed" — no one except himself would equate the Plague with the other dangers that he mentions. Such events as a battle, or a gale at sea, or a sandstorm are all widely recognized as having that quality which Burke called "the sublime" and Yeats "a terrible beauty." But the Plague has never aroused any reaction except repugnance and horror. The reason for this aesthetic distinction is that the Plague is encountered in a different way than these other dangers. War traditionally is thought of as something that men (and the rare woman) engage in voluntarily: for the sake of their country, or their religion, or, like Homer's heroes, simply for glory. Similarly, seafarers or travelers to remote and dangerous places such as mountains and deserts were thought of as willingly accepting the dangers involved; and it was this voluntary consent that created the perception of heroism. Arctic explorers who chose to go to the polar regions were seen as heroic; native peoples who faced the same difficult environment but not by choice were not.

But it is precisely this element of voluntary acceptance of risk which is missing in the Plague. Its danger falls impartially on the elderly, young adults, and children, and on men and women equally; it makes no distinction between combatant and civilian, or between the brave and the cowardly. Its particular horror lies in its indiscriminacy. (Similarly, as modern warfare has made death increasingly indiscriminate through the use of weapons of mass destruction and the widespread targeting of civilian populations, war has lost much of its traditional glamor and has come to be regarded more in the way the Plague is regarded.) Thus, when Walsingham proclaims, "So — for the Plague a hearty cheer!" what he is actually saying is, "The price of my having the satisfaction of demonstrating my courage in the face of possible death is that others, who are not interested in any such satisfaction and who wish to live, must suffer and die; and I accept that price." [1]

It is no wonder that the priest who enters at that moment responds to such a declaration with horror: "A godless feast, befitting godless madmen!" The priest, although he speaks in terms of traditional Christian doctrine, is less concerned about the relationship between God and man than the relationship between man and man. The feast implicitly denies the need for God by disrupting funeral services and the prayers for the dead; but the offense which the priest stresses is disregard not of God, but of the grief and suffering of the human mourners:

Your feasting and your shameless songs
Mock at and profane the gloomy peace
Spread everywhere by death and desolation!
Amidst the horror of the mournful burials,
Amidst pale faces I pray at the graveyard,
And your hateful shouts and cries of revelry
Disturb the silence of the tomb — because of you,
The earth itself trembles over the dead bodies!

Merriment in such circumstances, the priest goes on, is like the merriment of demons who openly rejoice in the sufferings of a damned soul. And just as godlessness and demonism are associated by the priest with indifference to others' suffering, so salvation is associated with human solidarity, with the preservation of emotional ties beyond even death: when the priest urges the revelers to disperse, he does not simply say, "if ever you hope to enter Heaven," but "if ever / You hope to meet again in Heaven / The souls of those whom you have lost."

The revelers' response shows that they are essentially a crowd of people each like the "young man," totally preoccupied with their own personal fear and their desire to seize any distraction from that fear, so that they refuse even to show any grasp of the ethical issue which the priest is raising; instead, they merely try to hoot him away. Only Walsingham is willing to confront the issue and to engage in a genuine dialogue with the priest, even if he comes down firmly against the priest's call for solidarity with the sufferers by his declaration, "youth loves gaiety."

Recognizing that he cannot reach the thoughtless crowd, the priest turns all his attention to Walsingham, addressing to him specifically the same message that was given in Mary's song, the survival of love after death and the continued concern of the dead for the living:

> Is that you, Walsingham? Are you the same man
> Who just three weeks ago dropped to your knees,
> Embracing your mother's body as you wept,
> And howling beat your fists upon her grave?
> Or do you think she isn't crying now,
> Shedding bitter tears in Heaven itself,
> To see her son caught up in reveling
> At a shameless feast, to hear your voice
> Singing like one possessed, amidst
> Holy prayers and deep-felt sighs?
> Follow me!

The priest's refusal to give up, his selfless determination to help Walsingham, enables the Chairman to recognizes in the priest what he has been unable to find in any of his shallow fellow revelers: someone capable of understanding an inner agony born, not of simple physical fear, but of spiritual desolation. Finding at last an equal, someone to whom he can speak, Walsingham pours out his heart in some of the most extraordinary lines in the "little tragedies," lines whose combination of beauty and devastation of spirit looks forward to Blok:

> Why have you come here
> To trouble me? I cannot, I must not
> Follow after you: I am bound here
> By despair, by terrible remembrance,
> By the knowledge of my lawlessness,
> And by the horror of that dead emptiness
> Which greets me now in my own house—
> And by the novelty of these furious revels,
> And by the blessed poison of this cup,
> And by the caresses—God forgive me—
> Of a being, ruined, but still dear . . .
> My mother's shade will not call me away
> From here—it's too late—I hear your voice
> Calling me—I recognize your striving
> To save me. . . . Old man, go in peace;
> But accursed may he be who follows you!

Walsingham acknowledges the justice of the priest's accusation against the revelers. He sees himself as "lawless," outside human society. His vocabulary echoes the priest's charge of demonism. He describes the revels as бешеных веселий, and while бешеный may mean simply "rabid, furious," its etymological meaning is "possessed by a demon (бес)." His reference to "the blessed poison of this cup" brings the feast very close to a blasphemous parody of the Communion service (the adjective I have translated as "blessed," благодатным, has a strong association with the receiving of grace; it is the epithet used after the words "Радуйся Дево" — "Rejoice, O Virgin" — in the Church Slavonic version of the *Ave Maria*). And his opening words to the priest, "Why have you come here / To trouble me?" combined with his final adjuration to the priest to leave him alone "in God's name" ("Зачем приходишь ты / Меня тревожить? . . . Отец мой, ради Бога, / Оставь меня") echo the demon's words to Christ in Mark 5:7: "What have You to do with me . . . ? I adjure You by God, do not torment me" ("Что Тебе до меня. . . ? Заклинаю Тебя Богом, не мучь меня").

But while Walsingham recognizes the correctness of the priest's diagnosis, he disputes the offered cure. For him, the memory of those who have loved him is not a comfort, but a torment, a "terrible remembrance"; the home that reminds him of them fills him with "horror." The "novelty" of the feast, its break with the past, is what draws him to it. And his reaction is not, as one might think, because he does not believe in the immortality of the soul, and thus wishes to put behind him a loss that he regards as irrecoverable. He is entirely willing to grant the priest's assertion that his mother's soul summons him away from the feast; but he will not go.

Why does Walsingham react to the memory of his past in this fashion? The play does not give us a direct answer, but its structure permits us to guess. Walsingham is a courageous man, but his courage is the courage of action, of challenging and defying an enemy. As Mary's song shows, this is not the only type of courage there is; the calmness with which Jenny contemplates her own death reminds us that enduring the inevitable with grace is also a form of courage. In a situation where this courage of endurance is required, it may indeed prove true, as Walsingham remarks apropos of Louisa's fainting, that "the cruel are weaker than the tender." Precisely because he is so proud of his own power, of his own active courage, Walsingham cannot withstand a blow which can only be endured, not fought — the loss of those close to him. The priest's question when reminding Walsingham of his paroxysm of grief at his mother's death—"Are you the same man / Who just three weeks ago dropped to your knees . . . ?"—is not simply a rhetorical one; Walsingham is at the feast precisely because he does not want to be "the same man," does not want to be humbled by so crushing a sorrow. But the only way that he can free himself from that pain is by dissociating himself from his memories of the dead. Thus his first response to the priest's exhortation, "Matilda's pure soul calls you!" is a furious demand for forgetfulness: he rises from the table and cries out

> Swear to me, lifting your pale
> And withered hand to Heaven, to leave
> That name forever silenced in the grave!

But in trying to deny or destroy his memories of those whom he loves, Walsingham is also destroying his own capability for love, for human sympathy; and the barren Titanism of the "Hymn to the Plague" is the result. He is fully aware of the spiritual damage he has inflicted upon himself, as indicated by the rest of his response to the mention of Matilda:

> Oh, if only I could hide this sight
> From her immortal eyes! Once
> She thought me pure, proud, free—
> And found paradise in my embrace . . .
> Where am I? Holy child of light! I see
> You there, where my fallen spirit
> Will never reach . . .

This passage illuminates his earlier affectionate reference to Mary—"a being, ruined, but still dear"—an affection based on Walsingham's perception of their similarity. Like Mary, Walsingham sees his life as broken apart, with an innocent, idyllic past that is separated by an impassible gulf from the corrupted present.

But is this actually the case? Walsingham speaks of his ruin in explicitly Christian terms — his wife, in Heaven, has become a "child of light" inaccessible to his "fallen spirit" — and yet the spokesman for Christianity, the priest, clearly does not regard Walsingham as irrecoverably lost. Instead, the priest calls upon Walsingham to save himself by repenting, in the original semantic sense of that word — to turn aside, to change his course. What Walsingham needs, and what the priest summons him to, is not the selfish, hollow "revelry" of the feast, but circumstances in which the wounds of his spirit can heal enough for him to be able to recognize his memories of those whom he has loved and lost not as a torment, but as a blessing — the "some place apart" where Jenny bids Edmund to "ease your weary heart" before returning to their village to visit her grave.[2] In his proud defiance, his unwillingness to accept loss and submit to grief, Walsingham deliberately refuses this possibility and rejects the salvation offered by the priest with the determined cry, "Father, for God's sake / Leave me!"

Walsingham chooses to remain at the feast. Instead of "dead emptiness . . . in my own house," he chooses the companionship of the table. And yet the society of the revelers is only a shell, a travesty, of a true society, of genuine human solidarity. That solidarity comes at the cost of bearing loss and grief, of remaining faithful to the memory of the dead. It is a cost that Walsingham recognizes, but is not willing to pay. "He who has not, even what little he has will be taken from him": even the sham society of the table is not left for Walsingham. His consciousness sets him apart from his fellow revelers, even as they have set themselves apart from the larger society. The feast goes on around him, but he is no longer a part of it. "The Chairman remains, plunged in deep contemplation."

Commentary

THE "MACRO" problems involved in translating the "little trage-dies," such as metrics or finding the right tone for a character's speech, have been discussed above. In addition, however, there are a number of "micro" problems—that is, difficulties in translating an individual word or phrase, whether because the Russian has overtones not re-producible in English, or because there are alternative translations for each of which a case could be made, or because avoiding a construc-tion which would be clumsy in English required taking some liberty in translation. What follows is a list of what I considered the most inter-esting or challenging "micro" problems, along with an explanation why a particular solution was chosen.

THE MISERLY KNIGHT

"Chenstone" is generally presumed to refer to the eighteenth-century English poet William Shenstone, who, however, did not write any work entitled *The Covetous Knight* (although some ideas that are echoed in Pushkin's play can be found in Shenstone's poem "Economy"). The subtitle is a deliberate mystification on Pushkin's part, apparently intended to emphasize the purely fictional nature of the work and thus discourage speculation about any real-life models for its characters.

This title is usually translated as *The Covetous Knight,* on the assumption that it was intended to correspond exactly to the English title of the fictitious "Chenstone" work. In fact, any Russian-English dictionary will translate the adjective скупой as "stingy, miserly" and скупость (the noun used by Albert in lines 36 and 136) as "stinginess, miserliness." Moreover, miserliness and covetousness are distinctly different qualities. Miserliness implies a great desire to acquire money, and an even greater desire not to part with it. Covetousness implies a desire to acquire something to which another has a rightful claim: "Thou shalt not covet thy neighbor's wife, nor his manservant, nor his maidservant, nor his ox, nor his ass, nor anything else that belongs to him." A miser could quite possibly also be a coveter, in the sense of wanting to add another's rightful wealth to his own hoard; but a coveter could just as well be a spendthrift. Clearly, the dominant characteristic of the baron is miserliness, not covetousness, and the title should reflect this.

This raises the question: why did Pushkin identify the nonexistent work that supposedly served as a basis for his play as *The Covetous Knight* rather than *The Miserly Knight?* One possibility, of course, is that Pushkin simply made a mistake in his English. However, there is also a more interesting possibility: that after having created a nonexistent English work to distance himself from imputations that his play was based on real life, he then wished to distance himself as well from the nonexistent English work. Hence the spelling of the author's name as Chenston (or Chenstone) — which suggests, but is not the same as, William Shenstone — and the description of this work as a "tragicomedy," whereas Pushkin's work is clearly a tragedy. Substituting "covetous" for "miserly" in the title of this nonexistent work would then be another way of producing this close-but-not-the-same effect.

Line 2: John: Pushkin — like Shakespeare, who did not hesitate to mix Danish names like Hamlet and Gertrude with the Latin name Polonius and the Greek (!) Laertes — seems to have been little concerned about the ethnic consistency of his characters' names. Albert has a Saxon name, but Pushkin's spelling of it, with the final "t" dropped, suggests that it should be pronounced as if it were French. The names of the other members of the nobility mentioned in the play are spelled (in transliteration from the Russian) as Delorzh, Clotilda, Remon, and Filip. In Latin letters these would presumably be Delorge, Clotild, Raymond, and Philip (or Philippe), suggesting a vaguely Franco-German location. The servant, however, is given the unmistakably Russian name Ivan. The most logical explanation would seem to be that, given the relatively insignificant position of this servant in terms of both his social status and his role in the play, Pushkin simply decided to give him a name which from the point of view of a Russian was as ordinary as possible. Turning Ivan into John preserved this "everyman" quality of his name in English.

Line 21. "Oh, this poverty!": the Russian is О бедность, бедность! which would translate literally as, "O poverty, poverty!": not something that I could imagine an English speaker saying. Nevertheless, the repetition does emphasize the degree of Albert's frustration.

Line 37. "Pah! It's not difficult to catch it here": the Russian is Да! заразаться здесь не трудно ею, which would literally translate as "Yes! It's not difficult . . ." But Albert's "da" is spoken not primarily to show agreement with anything previously said, but simply as an expression of contempt: its explosive sound (particularly as the first word in a sentence) is more important to his meaning than its dictionary definition.

Line 48. "Groaned and waffled." the Russian is Кряхтет да жмется, which A. F. B. Clark translates as "He sighed and shrugged." The difference lies in how hard one imagines John pressed for the loan. If John merely conveyed his master's request, Solomon would presumably have given him the equivalent of a coolly polite, "Gee, I'd like to help, but I can't" — in which case "sighed and shrugged" would be most accurate. If John had really been demanding about it, Solomon would probably have felt himself pushed into a corner, unwilling to say yes and not daring to say no — in which case he would have "groaned and waffled." Given Albert's hot-headedness, which could certainly take itself out on a servant who had failed to get a desired loan for him, it seemed likely to me that John pressed Solomon hard.

Line 124. "Poison too": the Russian is: "Твой старичок торгует ядом." "Да — и ядом." The "и" of "и ядом" is being used as a concession, a form of de-emphasis: "Well, yes, it is poison." My effort to convey this de-emphasis by "Poison too" (as if that were a normal part of commerce) was suggested by the literal definition of "и" as "and, also."

Line 200. "howling all the time": the Russian verb is воя, which means either "howling" (used to describe the sound of dogs or wolves) or "wailing." The former translation seemed to me more in keeping with the Baron's complete lack of sympathy for his petitioner.

Line 213. "I would suffocate": the Russian is я захлебнулся б, where the verb literally refers to choking on swallowed food, or by extension, to inability to get enough air (Nabokov translates it as ". . . and with a splutter/I'd perish in my trusty vaults"). The picture it calls up thus is not one of drowning, but of the Baron trapped in his vault by floodwaters outside, and dying as the air inside becomes exhausted.

Line 218. "tempered blade": the Russian is честной булат. A булат is a sword made of Damascus steel, highly prized during the Middle Ages; the adjectival form булатный is a standard poetic epithet for a sword. My translation is meant to indicate both the technical superiority of the weapon in question and the archaic, elevated quality of the language in which it is described.

Line 241. "With his hellraising friends out for a good time": the Russian is Развратников разгульных собеседник, more literally something like "A companion of wild/loose/debauched libertines/profligates" — a more explicit sexual reference than my suggestive "out for a good time." The Baron's eroticized view of his gold is echoed in his fear that it will fall into the hands of a sexual predator.

MOZART AND SALIERI

Line 3. "clear and simple as do-re-mi": the Russian is ясно, как простая гамма, literally "clear as a simple scale." However, while the Russian гамма is an obviously technical term whose reference to music is obvious, the English word "scale" has several possible meanings, of which the musical one is not necessarily the first to occur to a reader's or listener. Substituting "do-re-mi" for "scale" made the musical reference obvious and at the same time (courtesy of Rodgers and Hammerstein) comprehensible even to the nonmusical. The potential confusion over the English word "scale" has been noted by other translators who, however, have not fully solved the problem. Nabokov translates it as "plain as seven simple notes," which, if one does not know the underlying Russian, is somewhat perplexing: why should seven notes be plainer than, say, four or five? A clearer version is given by R. M. Hewitt, who translates this line as "simple as the scale of C." This makes the musical reference completely obvious; but it can be properly appreciated only by someone who realizes that C is the simplest scale to play on a piano (since it is the only one which does not require the use of black keys).

Line 66. "Who idly strolls through life": the Russian is Гуляки праздного, literally, "an idle stroller." The noun гуляки is from the same root as the verb гулять, "to go for a walk/stroll," or by extension, "to have a good time" (with an implication of partying or boisterousness). The adjective праздного is related to праздник, "holiday, festival" — a day when no work is done. This motif of Mozart's "idleness" will reappear in line 220, when Mozart describes artists as "happy idlers" — in Russian, счастливцев праздных.

Line 110. "my divineness is hungry": the Russian божество is a perfectly normal grammatical form meaning "godhead" or "divinity." However, the grammatical inappropriateness of "divineness" (along with its suggestion of a pun on the title "Highness") seemed to me more expressive of the playfully deflating nature of Mozart's statement.

Line 126: "Appearing like an angel": the Russian is Как некий херувим, literally, "Like a cherub." This, however, risked evoking the popular (and completely un-Scriptural) image of a cherub as a chubby-cheeked little child, while Salieri's speech makes it clear that he is envisioning the majesty of a heavenly messenger.

Line 158: "something has upset you?": the Russian is Ты . . . чем-нибудь расстроен? — a question with overtones that cannot be conveyed in English. The primary meaning of расстроен is indeed "upset," but bearing in mind Salieri's habit of expressing himself in musical terms, it is worth noting that it has a secondary meaning "out of tune." It also echoes Salieri's earlier theme of the apparent discrepancy between Mozart's personality and his music, since Salieri has praised the latter for its "just proportion" (стройность).

Line 174: "Greeted me respectfully": the Russian is Учтиво поклонившись. The Russian verb поклониться literally means "to bow," but is regularly used in the figurative sense "to greet" — a natural enough extension in a culture where bowing was a normal method of greeting someone. To a modern-day American, however, bowing is a somewhat exotic custom. As a result, if this line were translated as "Bowed to me respectfully," it would tend to catch the reader's or listener's attention — clearly not what Pushkin wanted, since in the Russian it is a subordinate clause. Translating it as the unremarkable "Greeted me respectfully" keeps the narrative free of this potential momentary distraction.

Lines 182–183. "Day and night my black man won't / Leave me alone": the Russian is Мне день и ночь покоя не дает / Мой черный человек, where черный человек can mean either "man (dressed) in black" or "black man." Mozart's sense that this черный человек is following him "like a shadow" indicates that his imagination has transformed the actual figure of the black-garbed man who commissioned the *Requiem* into a far more disturbing metaphysical figure, a personification of the "ghostly vision" of line 100, and accordingly I have used the ominously suggestive translation "black man."

Line 198. "too much a buffoon": the Russian is слишком был смешон, literally, "was too funny [a man]" or "was too droll [a man]." Although the derisive overtone of "buffoon" is not present in the Russian, it seemed to me to express the attitude toward humor that one would expect from a man as deadly serious (literally deadly) as Salieri.

Line 203. "to the faithful union": the Russian is за искренний союз. The normal meaning of искренний is "sincere, candid," which painfully underscores Salieri's act of treachery. But when referring to a union that links two people, the natural trait to emphasize would be its strength of commitment. Nabokov, apparently recognizing this problem, tried to include both the actual and the logically expected epithet: "the frank and loyal brotherhood." Unfortunately for his translation, "frank" has come to be associated with unwelcome sincerity — telling the truth at a time, or in a manner, which would not promote "brotherhood" — but the perception that the one epithet искренний should convey the double meaning of integrity and loyalty is a correct one. I chose "faithful" as the best single word I could think of to combine these concepts.

Line 210. "As if I had fulfilled a burdening duty": the Russian is Как будто тяжкий совершил я долг. The word долг means "debt" as well as "duty" (both are things which are "owed"), so that theoretically this line could be translated as "As if I had paid off a heavy debt." But given Salieri's concept of himself as a man with a mission — the one chosen by destiny to stop Mozart—it seems psychologically far more plausible for him to see himself as performing his duty.

Line 228. "That's not true": the Russian is Неправда. The Russian word правда means both "truth" and "justice." It is the word that Salieri uses in the first two lines of the play: "They say there's no justice [нет правды] here on earth / But there's no justice [правды нет] higher up, either." As it turns out, even when confronted with правда, Salieri proves unable to recognize it decisively, to distinguish between right and wrong.

Lines 229–231. "What of Michelangelo?": "[Pushkin's older contemporary] Karamzin stated in his *Letters of a Russian Traveller*, 'When tourists are shown Michelangelo's painting of the Crucifixion, they're always told that supposedly the artist, in order to be able to present the dying Christ realistically, killed the man who served as his model, but this story is totally unbelievable.' The [eighteenth-century] French poet [Antoine-Marin] Le Mierre, who recounted this legend in one of his works, added the observation: 'I cannot possibly believe that crime and genius can be combined.' " N. V. Kolosova (ed.), *Boldinskaya osen'* (Moscow: Molodaya gvardiya, 1982), p. 263. (Translation mine)

THE STONE GUEST

Line 10. "swaggering lord": the Russian is нахальный кавалер. Нахальство is the sort of unshakable belief in one's own right against everybody else, no matter what the situation, that leaves onlookers infuriated and at the same time experiencing a certain grudging admiration (the best translation might be "chutzpah"). In the context of a nobleman taking an evening stroll through a capital city, "swaggering" seemed to me the best expression of this self-assured, out-of-my-way approach to others.

Lines 16–17. "Don Juan violated his exile / And showed up in Madrid": the Russian is Дон Гуан из ссылки самовольно / В Мадрит явился, literally "Don Juan of his own self-will arrived in Madrid from exile." In the immediate context of the king's reaction, referring to Don Juan's return "of his own self-will" emphasizes the deliberate and criminal disregard of the royal will. My translation "violated his exile" was intended to suggest statutory language and thus point to the legal danger of Don Juan's position. In the larger context of the play, however, this phrase has an additional significance that is lost in translation: although Don Juan's constant claim is that he is driven by chance or did not plan what happened, the whole plot is set in motion by his "self-willed" choice of returning to Madrid.

Line 43. "A damned bad job": the Russian is Проклятая . . . должность. In view of Don Juan's fate, it is worth noting the repeated usage of the adjective проклятый, "damned" (in the theological sense), "accursed," which shows up also in line 122, "Damn this life" (more literally, "A damned life"—Проклятое житье); line 217, "Look, you damned fool" (гляли, проклятый); and line 231, "In a hellhole of an inn" (В проклятой венте).

Line 115. "He's bumped off the husband": the Russian is Мужа повалил, where повалил means something like "brought down" or "knocked over." "Bumped off" was the closest I could get to this strongly physical image.

Lines 131–132. "as if they were brought forth / Not from slavish memory": the Russian verb is рождала, "gave birth to"—Laura uses the same imagery of creative inspiration as birth as does Salieri in his first monologue.

Line 171. "Lucky man": the Russian is счастливец—the same word used by Don Juan to describe the knight-commander in lines 412 and 420. The adjective счастливый can mean either "happy" or "lucky"; I have chosen whichever sounded more natural in English in a given context.

Line 244. "How many times have you cheated on me": the Russian verb изменяла, "betrayed," is the one normally used for a spouse who commits adultery.

Line 306. "What do you want?": the Russian is чего вы требуете, literally, "what do you demand" — suggesting that Doña Anna is already aware of a compelling power in Don Juan's addresses to her.

Line 363. "What can I do for you?": the Russian is Что вам угодно, a standard phrase of politeness and service. Coming from Leporello, who is regularly insolent to his master (inevitably so, since no servant with any sense of decorum or propriety would take a position with Don Juan), this line would be appropriately delivered with an ironic overpoliteness.

Line 488. "Lovely being!": the Russian is Милое созданье; see the note on *A Feast During the Plague*, line 217, below.

Lines 532–533. "How importunate you are! . . . Oh, hide, Don Juan": in Russian, Какой ты неотвязчивый! . . . о скройся, Дон Гуан. Doña Anna has shifted from addressing Don Juan as "вы" (the formal "you," equivalent to the French "vous" or the German "Sie") to addressing him as "ты" (the intimate "you," equivalent to the French "tu" or the German "Du"). This verbal shift is even more of a surrender to Don Juan than her kiss, since in nineteenth-century Russia, a woman would address a mere suitor as "вы"; "ты" would imply the existence or anticipation of a sexual relationship.

Line 540. "The stony grip of his right hand": the Russian is Пожатье каменной его десницы, "the grip of his stone right hand." Десница or десная (right hand) is an archaic form typically used to refer to divine action: десница провидения (the hand of Providence), овцы о десную, козлища о шую ("the sheep on the right hand, the goats on the left" — referring to God's division of humanity into the righteous and unrighteous at the Last Judgment, as described in Matthew 25:31–46). Thus the use of the word десница to refer to the hand that drags Don Juan to his doom suggests the supernatural nature of the retribution involved.

Line 541. "Let go — let go of me": the Russian is пусти, пусти мне руку, literally, "let go, let go of my hand." I have omitted the word "hand" because it is contextually obvious that it is Don Juan's hand that the statue is holding on to; because including the word would echo the word "hand" in a way which does not occur in the original, which distinguishes "десницы" used in the line before and "руку" used here; and because "let go, let go of my hand" is accentually clumsy (let gó, let gó of my hánd) compared to "let go, let go of me" (let gó, let gó of mé).

A FEAST DURING THE PLAGUE

Given the absence of articles in Russian, the first problem for a translator of this play is whether its title, Пир во время чумы, should be translated as *A Feast in Time of Plague* or *A Feast in the Time of the Plague*. The former translation implies an "outside" or "God's-eye" view of the Plague as a recurring and unsurprising phenomenon in human history (as a prayer to be read "in time of war" implies the expectation that such a prayer will be needed by successive generations). "The time of the Plague," by contrast, suggests how it would be seen by a person living through it: there was a normal time, and then a violent disruption, and then—for the survivors—something like normality again; this disruption was "the Plague," as survivors of a war would speak of it as "the war." Since Pushkin's play emphasizes, not the phenomenon of Plague as it has affected human beings throughout history, but the response of a number of individuals to the deadly threat which has disrupted their former lives, the appropriate choice would be with articles—*A Feast in the Time of the Plague*. This phrase, however, is clumsy sounding in English, and the substitution *A Feast During the Plague* naturally suggests itself (as it did, for example, to Mirsky in his *A History of Russian Literature*).

Lines 17–18. "Although that tongue of wondrous eloquence / Has not yet fallen silent in the grave": the Russian is Хотя красноречи-вейший язык / Не умолкал еще во прахе гроба. These lines seem to have caused some confusion among translators: Werth makes them read, "But mark you, his most eloquence discourses / Continued almost to the very last," while Nabokov gives, "Though never was so eloquent a tongue / doomed to keep still in a decaying casket." The source of the problem emerges when comparing Pushkin's text with Wilson's. Wilson reads: "His chair stands / Empty at your right hand— as if expecting / That jovial wassailer—but he is gone / Into cold narrow quarters. Well, I deem / The grave did never silence with its dust / A tongue more eloquent; but since 'tis so, / And store of boon companions yet survive, / There is no reason to be sorrowful." Pushkin's translation reverses Wilson's image—the dust of the grave has *not* silenced the dead man's eloquent tongue. This reversal is in keeping with the dominant issue of Pushkin's play, the theme of the continuing communion between the living and the dead. As a result of this reversal, while Wilson's lines form a continuous exposition, Pushkin's lines 17–18 are disjoined from the ones which follow them. Werth and Nabokov apparently felt this disjunction and, not realizing its larger significance, tried to find translations which would smooth it over.

Line 27. "with rude perfection": the Russian is с диким совершенством, where дикий literally means "wild," natural, uncultivated—emphasizing the "primitive" quality of the performance, and thus its appropriateness to folk music. The use of "rude" in the somewhat paradoxical-sounding translations both in this line and in line 79 ("rude paradise"—дикий рай) is intended to suggest Walsingham's combination of attraction to and skepticism towards the "noble savage" cliche of Scottish rural life.

Lines 104–105 (stage direction). "A black man is driving": the Russian is Негр управляет ею. Негр is a cognate of "Negro," but in keeping with common usage, I have translated it as "black man." It must, however, be understood that this "black man" is a man with black skin, as opposed to the "black man" (man dressed in black, черный человек of *Mozart and Salieri*.

Lines 118–119. "although the street's all ours, / An untrafficked hiding-place from death": the Russian is хотя улица вся наша / Безмолвное убежнище от смерти, literally, "although all our street / Is a silent refuge from death." Безмолвное, however, means "silent" in the specific sense of "lacking the sound of human voices"—for an urban street, a profoundly abnormal and disturbing condition. "An untrafficked hiding-place" reflects this implication of plague-stricken desolation.

Lines 156–161. The fourth stanza of Walsingham's song: the Russian is Есть упоение в бою, / И бездны мрачной на краю, / И в разъяренном океане, / Средь грозных волн и бурной тьмы, / И в аравийское урагане, / И в дуновении Чумы. which translates literally as: "There is intoxication in battle, / And on the edge of a gloomy abyss, / And on the infuriated ocean / Among threatening waves and stormy darkness / And in the Arabian hurricane / And in the breath of the Plague." In line 157, for the sake of rhyme ("flight/height") I have changed the observer's perspective slightly, since Walsingham's lyrics suggest an observer standing on the edge of a cliff looking down, rather than atop a mountain; but the sense of a vast space open beneath the observer is the same. In line 160, in recognition of the fact that Arabia no longer evokes the same exotic and forbidden aura that it would have had for a European in 1830, I have moved the "Arabian hurricane"—more pedantically, a sandstorm—to the unquestionably fearsome terrain of the Sahara.

Line 166. "And blest is he": the Russian is И счастлив тот, where счастлив would more accurately be translated as "happy" (unlike "blest," it has no theological overtone).

Line 188. "to outer darkness": the original is в тьму кромешную, an echo of the Church Slavonic Gospels; I have used the equivalent phrase from the King James Version (Matt. 22:13).

Line 217. "Of a being, ruined, but still dear": the Russian is Погибшего, но милого созданья, "of a lost but dear creature." However, "creature" has an overtone of contempt in English, particularly when applied to a prostitute, which Pushkin clearly did not intend to have in the Russian, since the same phrase (Милое созданье) is used by Don Juan in addressing Doña Anna. Thus in both cases I have translated созданье as "being." Милое suggests something which evokes love or is worthy of being loved; the word "dear," used here, would be a standard translation. In *The Stone Guest*, however, "dear" seemed a distinctly weak epithet for an impassioned love speech, and so, by an extension of the idea of loveableness, I translated it as "lovely."

Notes

1. The phrase "little tragedies" was used by Pushkin in a letter to P.A.
Pletnev dated 9 December 1830, in which Pushkin, while enumerating the
works he had written at Boldino, describes the four plays as "several dramatic
scenes, or little tragedies" ("несколько драматических сцен, или
маленьких трагедий").

2. In a letter to Mme. Goncharova dated 5 April 1830, Pushkin wrote, "Only
habit and long intimacy could enable me to gain the affection of Mlle. your
daughter; I may hope that she will become attached to me over time, but I
have nothing to offer that would please her; if she consents to give me her
hand, I would regard it only as proving the tranquil indifference of her heart.
But surrounded by admiration, homages, temptations, will her tranquillity
endure? People will tell her that only an unhappy fate prevented her from

making another match, more equal, more brilliant, more worthy of her—those comments will perhaps be sincere, and certainly she will think them so. Will she not have regrets? Will she not see me as an obstacle, a fraudulent abductor? Will she not come to detest me? God is my witness that I am ready to die for her, but to have to die and leave her a dazzling widow, free to choose a new husband the next day—that idea is hell." (In the original French: "L'habitude et une longue intimité pourraient seules me faire gagner l'affection de M-lle votre fille; je puis espérer me l'attacher à la longue, mais je n'ai rien pour lui plaire; si elle consent à me donner sa main, je n'y verrai que la preuve de la tranquille indifférence de son coeur. Mais entourée d'admiration, d'hommages, de séductions, cette tranquillité lui durera-t-elle? On lui dira qu'un malheureux sort l'a seul empêchée de former d'autres liens plus égaux, plus brillants, plus dignes d'elle,—peut-être ces propos seront-ils sincères, mais à coup sûr elle les croira tels. N'aura-t-elle pas des regrets? ne me regardera-t-elle pas comme un obstacle, comme un ravisseur frauduleux? ne me prendra-t-elle pas en aversion? Dieu m'est témoin que je suis prêt à mourir pour elle, mais devoir mourir pour la laisser veuve brillante et libre de choisir demain un nouveau mari—cette idée—c'est l'enfer.")

3. D. S. Mirsky, *A History of Russian Literature from Its Beginnings to 1900* (New York: Vintage Books, 1958), p. 101.

THE "LITTLE TRAGEDIES" IN ENGLISH: *An Approach*

1. The published translations of the "little tragedies" with which I am familiar are Eugene M. Kayden's translation of all four plays (Yellow Springs, Ohio: Antioch Press, 1965); A. F. B. Clark's *The Covetous Knight, Mozart and Salieri,* and *The Stone Guest* in *The Works of Alexander Pushkin: Lyrics, Narrative Poems, Folk Tales, Plays, Prose,* edited and with an introduction by Avrahm Yarmolinsky (New York: Random House, 1936); Vladimir Nabokov's translation of the Baron's second-scene monologue from *The Covetous Knight* and the complete texts of *A Feast During the Plague* and *Mozart and Salieri,* printed in *Three Russian Poets: Selections from Pushkin, Lermontov and Tyutchev* (Norfolk, Conn.: New Directions, 1944); James E. Falen's translations of *Mozart and Salieri* and *The Stone Guest* in *The Pushkin Journal,* vols. 1 (1993) and 2 (1994) respectively; R. M. Hewitt's *Mozart and Salieri* (Nottingham: University College, 1938); and Alexander Werth's *A Feast in the City of the Plague* in *Slavonic Review,* 6, no. 16 (June 1927).

2. T. S. Eliot, *Poetry and Drama* (London: Faber & Faber L., 1951), pp. 12–13.

3. Ibid., p. 15.

4. Eliot, *The Music of Poetry* (Glasgow: Jackson, Son & Company, 1942), pp. 19–21.

5. Ibid., pp. 21–22.

6. In the original Russian:

"Я стараюсь. . .насколько возможно, быть верным оригиналу, но только там, где верность или точность не вредит художественному впечатлению, и, ни минуты не колеблясь, я отделяюсь от подстрочности, если это может дать на русском языке другое впечатление, чем по-немецки.

"Я думаю, что не следует переводить слова и даже иногда смысл, а главное, надо передавать впечатление.

"Необходимо, чтобы читатель перевода переносился бы в ту же сферу, в которой находится читатель оригинала, и чтобы перевод действовал на те же нервы." Kornei Chukovskii, *Vysokoe iskusstvo* (Moscow: Sovetskii pisatel', 1988), p. 81.

7. In the original Russian: "Каким размером, например, переводить узбеками стихотворения Лермонтова, если четырехстопный ямб для них экзотика, совершенно чуждая их стиховому мышлению? Тут никакая эквиритмия немыслима, потому что в богатой, утонченной и сложной поэтической традиции узбеков четырехстопному ямбу нет места, и узбеки, которые в течение многих столетий накопили огромный поэтический опыт, воспринимают европейскую форму стиха совершенно иначе, чем мы. Когда пришлось, например, перевести на узбекский язык лермонтовского 'Хаджи Абрека,' два замечательных узбекских поэта, Гафур Гулям и Шейх-заде, даже и не пытался передать его тем же размером. Ибо для узбекского уха это не было эквивалентом того впечатления, которое тот же ямб доставляет нашему русскому уху. Поэтому Гафур Гулям перевел четырехстопный лермонтовский ямб тринадцатисложным 'бармаком' (то есть силлабическим размером), а Шейх-заде— девятисложным 'бармаком,' и на традиционном фоне узбекской поэзии это и является эквивалентом четырехстопного ямба." Ibid., p. 77.

8. In the original French: "La vraisemblance des situations et la vérité du dialogue—voilà la véritable règle de la tragédie. (Je n'ai pas lu Calderon ni Vega) mais quel homme que ce Sch.<akespeare>! je n'en reviens pas. Comme Byron le tragique est mesquin devant lui! . . . Lisez Sch.<akespeare>, il ne craint jamais de compromettre son personnage, il le fait parler avec tout l'abandon de la vie, car il est sûr en temps et lieu de lui faire trouver le langage de son caractère."

9. All of the ballads mentioned in the following discussion are well-known ones that have been reprinted many times. One book that conveniently contains all of them is *The Oxford Book of Ballads*, ed. Arthur Quiller-Couch (Oxford: Clarendon Press, 1927).

THE SEDUCTION OF POWER: *The Miserly Knight*

1. A. G. Gukasova, *Boldinskii period v tvorchestve Pushkina* (Moscow: Prosveshchenie, 1973), p. 81.

BETRAYAL OF A CALLING: *Mozart and Salieri*

1. In the original Russian: "В первое представление *Дон Жуана*, в то время когда весь театр, полный изумленных знатоков, безмольно упивался гармонией Моцарта, раздался свист—все обратились с негодованием, и знаменитый Сальери вышел из залы—в бешенстве, снедаемый завистью . . . Завистник, который мог освистать Д.⟨он⟩ Ж.⟨уана⟩, мог отравить его творца." A. S. Pushkin, *Polnoe sobranie sochinenii* (Moscow: Voskresenie, 1994–1997), v. 11, p. 218. Pushkin appears to have been misled by an inaccurate secondary source. The world premiere of *Don Giovanni* (in Prague) was indeed received with great enthusiasm, but Salieri was not in Prague at the time. It is entirely possible that he attended the Vienna (Court) premiere of the work; but its reception at Vienna was decidedly mixed, so that the dramatic incident of one heckler against the whole house could not have happened.

2. S. V. Rassadin, *Dramaturg Pushkin. Poetika. Idei. Evoliutsiia* (Moscow: Iskusstvo, 1977), p. 124.

3. For a discussion of this "Luciferian" imagery, see Robert Louis Jackson, "Miltonic Imagery and Design in Puškin's *Mozart and Salieri:* The Russian

Satan," in *American Contributions to the Seventh International Congress of Slavists,* ed. Victor Terras (The Hague, 1973), pp. 261–270.

4. V. Vatsuro, in *"Moʒart i Sal'eri," tragediia Pushkina. Dviʒhenie vo vremeni,* Pushkin v XX veke, III (Moscow: Nasledie, 1977), p. 720.

THE WEIGHT OF THE PAST: *The Stone Guest*

1. In the original Russian: "Живая, кипучая, торжествующая жизнь, олицетворенная в образе Дон Гуана, все время омрачается 'виденьем гробовым'—неотступно возникающим призраком смерти . . . Но жизнь не только все время дается в пьесе рядом, бок о бок со смертью. Жизнь бросает вызов смерти . . . в особенности,—в приглашении Дон Гуаном статуи командора охранять его любовную встречу с Доной Анной. И на всем протяжении пьесы жизнь торжествует. Только в самом конце смерть оказывается победительницей, но и тут она, как в опере Моцарта, не в силах сломить дух Дон Гуана." D. D. Blagoi, *Tvorcheskii put' Pushkina. 1826–1830* (Moscow: Sovetskii pisatel', 1967), p. 658.

2. In the original Russian: "Именно живого человеческого чувства не может простить Дон Гуану мертвый и бездушный мир . . . Барон погиб оттого, что *перестал* быть человеком, теперь же 'жестокий век' мстит Дон Гуану за то, что в нем *пробудился* человеком." D. Ustiuzhanin, *Malen'kie tragedii A. S. Pushkina* (Moscow: Khudozhestvennaya literatura, 1974), pp. 82, 83; italics in original.

3. "Наказание без преступления." In: S. V. Rassadin, *Dramaturg Pushkin. Poetika. Idei. Evoliutsiia.* Moscow: Iskusstvo, 1977.

4. Frank Seeley, "The Problem of *Kamennyj Gost',*" *Slavonic and East European Review,* 41 (1963), pp. 362, 354.

5. Richard Gregg, "The Eudaemonic Theme in Puškin's 'Little Tragedies,'" *Alexander Puškin: A Symposium on the 175th Anniversary of His Birth,* ed. Andrej Kodjak and Kiril Taranovsky (New York: New York University Press, 1976), pp. 189, 194.

6. In the original Russian: "К своему светлому зениту Дон Гуан шел порочным путем (как Барон и Сальери—ведь они тоже думали, что преследуют высокие цели), шел . . . на каждому шагу нарушая не столько божеские, сколько человеческие законы,

подчиняя все своему 'я хочу'. Цепь 'преступлений' Дон Гуана завершилась приглашением Командора. Каков бы ни был Командор, поступок Дон Гуана — глумление, издевательство, унижение человека, пусть мертвого, и оскорбление его вдовы. Простить этого нельзя." V. Nepomniashchii, "O malen'kikh tragediiakh," *Malen'kie tragedii* (Moscow: Iskusstvo, 1967), pp. 75–76.

7. Charles Corbet, "L'originalité du *Convive de pierre* de Pouchkine," *Revue de littérature comparée,* 29, no. 1 (1955), pp. 52–54, points out two similarities between Villiers's play and Pushkin's: the plot device of Don Juan's disguising himself as a monk, and the mention of the knight-commander's name as Don Alvaro (a name that occurs in no pre-Pushkin version except Villiers's). Pushkin might independently have come up with the idea of a clerical disguise, but it seems highly unlikely that pure chance would lead him to pick exactly the same fairly uncommon Christian name for his knight-commander.

8. This translation is given in Walter Arndt, *Pushkin Threefold: Narrative, Lyric, Polemic and Ribald Verse; The Originals with Linear and Metric Translations* (New York: E. P. Dutton, 1972), p. 32. The Russian original is: "Воспоминание безмолвно предо мной / Свой длинный развивает свиток; / И с отвращением читая жизнь мою, / Я трепещу и проклинаю, / И горько жалуюсь, и горько слезы лью, / Но строк печальных не смываю."

SURVIVAL AND MEMORY: *A Feast During the Plague*

1. It is worth comparing Walsingham's attitude toward the Plague with that described in Pushkin's poem "The Hero" ("Герой"), which was also written at Boldino in 1830. In "The Hero," which takes the form of a dialogue between a poet and his friend, the poet says that, out of all of Napoleon's acts, the one that most captivates his imagination is the legend that during his Middle Eastern campaign, the future emperor visited his plague-stricken soldiers in a field hospital and unhesitatingly touched their hands — a degree of fearlessness worthy of Walsingham's hymn. But what makes this gesture heroic, in the poet's eyes, is not merely the degree of fearlessness it shows, but the fact that it was performed to give comfort and courage to the desperately sick men. It is this compassion, the poet asserts, which makes the

difference between a hero and a tyrant. By contrast, compassion for the stricken is completely lacking in Walsingham's fearlessness.

2. The connection between Walsingham and the bereaved Edmund is rightly made by Donald Loewen, "Disguised as Translation: Religion and Re-creation in Pushkin's *A Feast in Time of Plague*," *Slavic and East European Journal*, 40, no. 1 (1996), pp. 50–51.

Select Bibliography

Akhmatova, Anna. *"Kamennyi gost'* Pushkina (Pushkin's *The Stone Guest*)."
  Sochineniia, ed. G. P. Struve and B. A. Fillipov. Vol. 2. Munich:
  Inter-Language Library Associates, 1968.
Alexandrov, Vladimir E. "Correlations in Pushkin's *Malen'kie tragedii.*"
  Canadian Slavonic Papers, 20 (1978): 176–193.
Bayley, John. *Pushkin: A Comparative Commentary.* Cambridge: Cambridge
  University Press, 1971.
Bidney, Martin. "Thinking about God and Mozart: the Salieris of Puškin and
  Peter Shaffer." *Slavic and East European Journal,* 30, no. 2 (1986): 183–195.
Blagoi, D. D. *Tvorcheskii put' Pushkina. 1826–1830 (Pushkin's Artistic Path,
  1826–1830).* Moscow: Sovetskii pisatel', 1967.
Chukovskii, Kornei. *Vysokoe iskusstvo.* Moscow: Sovetskii pisatel', 1988.
  (Available in English as *The Art of Translation: Kornei Chukovsky's*

"A High Art." Tr. and ed. Lauren G. Leighton. Knoxville: University of Tennessee Press, 1984.)

Corbet, Charles. "L'originalité du *Convive de pierre* de Pouchkine." *Revue de Littérature Comparée,* 29, no. 1 (1955): 48–71.

Darskii, D. *Malen'kiia tragedii Pushkina (Pushkin's "Little Tragedies").* Moscow, 1915.

Durylin, S. N. *Pushkin na stsene (Staging Pushkin's Plays).* Moscow: Izdatel'stvo Akademii nauk SSSR, 1951.

Eliot, T. S. *The Music of Poetry: The Third W. P. Ker Memorial Lecture Delivered in the University of Glasgow 24th February 1942.* Glasgow: Jackson, Son & Company, 1942.

———. *Poetry and Drama: The Theodore Spencer Memorial Lecture, Harvard University, November 21, 1950.* London: Faber & Faber, 1951.

Ermakov, I. D. *Etiudy po psikhologii tvorchestva A. S. Pushkina. Opyt organicheskogo ponimaniia "Domik v Kolomne," "Proroka" i malen'kikh tragedii (Studies in the Artistic Psychology of A. S. Pushkin: Towards an Organic Understanding of "The Little House in Kolomna," "The Prophet," and the Little Tragedies).* Psikhologicheskaia i psikhoanaliticheskaia biblioteka pod. red. prof. I. D. Ermakova. Moscow, 1923.

Gifford, H. "Puškin's *Feast in Time of Plague* and Its Original." *American Slavic and East European Review,* 7 (1949): 37–46.

Gregg, Richard. "The Eudaemonic Theme in Puškin's 'Little Tragedies.'" In *Alexander Puškin: A Symposium on the 175th Anniversary of His Birth,* ed. Andrej Kodjak and Kiril Taranovsky. New York: New York University Press, 1976.

———. "Pushkin and Shenstone: The Case Reopened." *Comparative Literature,* 17, no. 2 (spring 1965): 109–116.

Gukasova, A. G. *Boldinskii period v tvorchestve Pushkina (Pushkin's Boldino Period).* Moscow: Prosveshchenie, 1973.

Jackson, Robert L. "Miltonic Imagery and Design in Puškin's *Mozart and Salieri:* The Russian Satan." *American Contributions to the Seventh International Congress of Slavists,* ed. Victor Terras. Vol. 2. The Hague: Mouton, 1973.

———. "Moral-Philosophical Subtext in Pushkin's *Kamennyi gost'.*" *Scando-Slavica,* 35 (1989): 17–24.

Karpiak, Robert. "Pushkin's *Little Tragedies:* The Controversies in Criticism." *Canadian Slavonic Papers,* 22 (1980): 80–91.

Lesskis, G. A. "*Kamennyi gost'.* Tragediia gedonizma" (*The Stone Guest:* The Tragedy of Hedonism). *Pushkin. Issledovaniia i materialy* 13 (1989): 134–145.

Loewen, Donald. "Disguised as Translation: Religion and Re-creation in Pushkin's *A Feast in Time of Plague.*" *Slavic and East European Journal,* 40, no. 1 (1996): 45–62.

Mirsky, D. S. *A History of Russian Literature from Its Beginnings to 1800.* New York: Vintage Books, 1958.

Nepomniashchii, V. S., comp. "*Mozart i Sal'eri,*" tragediia Pushkina. Dvizhenie vo vremeni (*Pushkin's Tragedy "Mozart and Salieri": Movement in Time*). Pushkin v XX veke, III. Moscow: Nasledie, 1977. A chronologically arranged collection of 65 studies of the play written by prominent Russian scholars, beginning in the mid-nineteenth century and ending in the 1990s.

———. "O malen'kikh tragediiakh" (The 'Little Tragedies'). In: Alexander Pushkin, *Malen'kie tragedii.* Moscow: Iskusstvo, 1967.

Pushkin, Alexander. *Boldinskaia osen'. Stikhotvoreniia, poemy, malen'kie tragedii, povesti, skazki, pis'ma, kriticheskie stat'i, napisannye A. S. Pushkinym v sele Boldino Lukoianovskogo uezda Nizhegorodskoi gubernii osen'iu 1830 goda (The Boldino Autumn: Lyric and Narrative Poems, "Little Tragedies," Short Stories, Folk Tales, Letters, and Critical Articles Written by A. S. Pushkin in Boldino . . . in Autumn 1830).* Ed. N. V. Kolosova. Moscow: Molodaia gvardiia, 1982.

———. "A Feast in the City of the Plague." Trans. Alexander Werth. *Slavonic Review,* 6, no. 16 (June 1927): 17–184.

———. *Little Tragedies.* Translated from the Russian by Eugene M. Kayden, illustrated by Vladimir Favorsky. Yellow Springs, Ohio: Antioch Press, 1965.

———. "Mozart and Salieri." Trans. James E. Falen. *The Pushkin Journal,* 1, no. 2 (1993): 228–249.

———. *Mozart and Salieri.* Trans. R. M. Hewitt. Translations from the Russian, I. Nottingham: University College, 1938.

———*Polnoe sobranie sochinenii. Tom VII, Dramaticheskie proizvedeniia (Complete Works. Volume 7: Dramatic Works).* Vol. 7, ed. V. P. Iakubovich.

Moscow: Akademiia nauk, 1935. No other volume of this set was ever published.

―――. *Polnoe sobranie sochinenii (Complete Works)*. Ed. V. D. Bonch-Bruevich. Moscow: Voskresenie, 1994–1997.

―――. *Pushkin Threefold: Narrative, Lyric, Polemic, and Ribald Verse; The Originals with Linear and Metric Translations by Walter Arndt*. New York: E. P. Dutton, 1972.

―――. "The Stone Guest." Trans. James E. Falen. *The Pushkin Journal*, 2–3 (1994–1995): 55–129.

―――. *Three Russian Poets: Selections from Pushkin, Lermontov, and Tyutchev, in New Translations by Vladimir Nabokov*. The Poets of the Year. Norfolk, Conn.: New Directions, 1944.

―――. *The Works of Alexander Pushkin: Lyrics, Narrative Poems, Folk Tales, Plays, Prose*. Selected and edited, with an introduction, by Avrahm Yarmolinsky. New York: Random House, 1936.

Quiller-Couch, Arthur, ed. *The Oxford Book of Ballads*. Oxford: Clarendon Press, 1927.

Rassadin, S. V. *Dramaturg Pushkin. Poetika. Idei. Evoliutiia (Pushkin's Dramaturgy: Poetics, Ideas, Evolution)*. Moscow: Iskusstvo, 1977.

Seeley, Frank. "The Problem of *Kamennyj Gost'*." *Slavonic and East European Review*, 41 (1963): 346–367.

Terras, Victor. "Puškin's *Feast During the Plague* and Its Original: A Structural Confrontation." In *Alexander Puškin: A Symposium on the 175th Anniversary of His Birth*, ed. Andrej Kodjak and Kiril Taranovsky. New York: New York University Press, 1976.

Tomashevskii, Boris. "Malen'kie tragedii Pushkina i Mol'er" (Pushkin's 'Little Tragedies' and Molière). *Pushkin. Vremennik pushkinskoi kommissii*. Tom 1. Moscow: Izdatel'stvo Akademii nauk, 1936–1941.

Ustiuzhanin, D. *Malen'kie tragedii A. S. Pushkina (Pushkin's 'Little Tragedies')*. Moscow: Khudozhestvennaia literatura, 1974.

Wilson, John. *The City of the Plague*. Edinburgh: Printed by G. Ramsay and Company for A. Constable and Company, 1816.

Index

Other volumes in the Russian Literature and Thought Series

891.723 Pushkin, Aleksandr
PUS   Sergeevich, 1799-
           1837.

           The little
           tragedies.

$13.00

DATE			